ABOUT THE AUTHOR

Thakur Shailendra Nath was born in the year 1959 in Sitamarhi District of Bihar in an agriculturist family. He has graduated from Ranchi University and presently serving in Customs & Central Excise Department in M.P. He has written several books and his many articles have been published in prominent national magazines. His other books on White Collar Crime, Environment, Marketing of Agricultural Products and Interlinking of All India Rivers has been widely appreciated.

Sitamarhi, being the actual birth place of Sita, from very child hood he has closely observed, felt and experienced the old traditions which are still prevalent in the Mithila region. His thoughts and memories stored in his mind have come out in this way.

Sita:

The Great Daughter of King Janaka of Mithila

Thakur Shailendra Nath

Originals
Delhi

First Published 2014

ISBN 13: 978-81-8454-139-7
ISBN 10: 81-8454-139-2

Published By
Originals
A-6, Second Floor, Nimri Commercial Centre,
Ashok Vihar Phase-4, Delhi - 110 052 (India)
Tel.: +91 11 2730 2453 Fax: 011 4706 1936
website: www.Lppindia.com
e-mail: info@Lppindia.com

Printed At
D K Fine Art Press P Ltd.
Delhi-110052

PRINTED IN INDIA

Contents

Preface

I am pleased to present my latest book titled "Sita: The Great Daughter of King Janak of Mithila" before the readers. Much has already been written on the Goddess Sita and there is hardly any aspect untouched, yet this is a small effort from a small writer paying respect to the Goddess. Mithila is a land of Gods and rivers where rivers are continuously enriching its soil from the age old period. Every pious soul desire to spend his last time in Mithila to get salvation. This beauty of Mithila cannot be described only it can be experienced when one stays here for some time.

Ramayan is a great epic, many versions of Ramayan exist but the most popular one are Ramcharitmanas by Tulsidas and Ramayan by Valmiki. It is believed that Valmiki's Ramayan is the original one and all other versions were written after that. Tulsidas was devotee of Ram and he wrote Ramayan as devotee, so obviously he didn't find any fault with Ram and his actions, he projects Sita as very devoted and obedient wife, his version is more religious whereas original Valmiki's version is more secular in nature may be because he wrote as a contemporary not as a devotee. Sita is obedient, devoted, submissive wife, who follows her husband wherever he goes, suffers silently without protesting. Or is it independent, courageous, bold, fearless, powerful Sita who fought with her husband to accompany him to forest, faced aggressive and powerful Ravan, raised her kids as a single mother, refused to go back to her husband after he deserted her? Today Sita is only looked as a loyal, faithful, devoted women or wife her liberal, fearless and independent nature is conveniently ignored.

Whenever we want to look for any ideals we always tend to look into past as if there are no role models in today's world. Actually there are many role models in today's world to whom we can relate very easily, who are living or lived in similar conditions in which we are living today. We expect that texts written long ago, in totally different era and time will have relevance in all aspects even today. Mythology and these texts or epics are fascinating for number of reasons, they teach us many valuable lessons but to expect them to provide answers for all our problems in modern world might be expecting too much from them. We don't live in the same era in which these texts were written so why we expect to find all those values in today's world. Some people advocate that we should totally get over these myths and beliefs but I don't think it's possible, their hold on society and our culture is so strong that it is impossible to ignore them. We should use them in positive manner rather than using it for selfish purpose as per our convenience or to suppress certain class.

Today's women face different challenges than Sita or Draupadi faced in times of Ramayan or Mahabharat, both these women had difficulties in their lives and fought their way out. There might be some similarity in certain situations but value system and society structure is totally different today, so may be Sita and Draupadi can not provide all the motivation necessary for modern women to excel. Whenever Sita's example is revoked, most of the time it is with intention to tell women that they should behave in very polite, obedient manure and follow their husbands' instructions without any protest, as Sita does in Ramcharitmanas. Its always with intention to constrain them to show their boundries and to remind them that they should not cross so called Lakshman Rekha. Valmiki's projection of Sita's character is very strong character compared to Tulsidas's but people conveniently ignore strong characteristics of Sita's personality and only try to project her as obedient and faithful wife, which is very limited representation of her total personality.

One aspect of Hinduism life is that it allows to have many versions of truth. It doesn't project world in either good or bad (black or white). It says that good can become bad and bad can also become good, there is lot of grey in world and many times its very difficult to differentiate good from bad. Today people are trying to jacket Hinduism to give it particular look, people want to see heroes and villains in men, they see either goddesses or whores in women there is nothing in between. May be ideal man or woman is a myth, which we only see in books or movies.

Society is not static, it changes over time. Even though content of books might remain same, its understanding and interpretations changes over time, every era interprets them differently. Many times people who think they are in-charge of religion or consider these books as a property of certain religion or sect try to freeze opinions, they insist that these books which were written long ago, in totally different time and era should be interpreted in same way as they were interpreted thousands of years ago. They even insist that they are all relevant even in today's world also, any objection or different interpretation of these books is heavily criticized or even criminalized. Whether people like it or not, every generation will interpret and understand these books according to their own need, requirement and judge them accordingly. If we want to get inspirations from these books then let us take all positive things and try to leave the stuff which is no longer relevant in today's world. This won't dilute the impact of these books, it's characters or its not their insult, its proof of their greatness that we still study them and use them as one of our guides. May be Sita from Ramcharitmanas is not very ideal example for modern women to follow but many of her qualities like fearlessness, faithfulness, independent nature are certainly useful even today, Sita of Valmiki's Ramayan lived very independent life and women today also want to live independent life, so there are many similarities and we all can take lot of inspiration from her. Let society or that particular individual decide what he/she want to become, whom they want to follow, advice should be offered whenever it's required but let people have freedom to accept or reject it. Let us stop using these characters as per our own convenience for our selfish motives, lets study them so that we can learn what they actually want to teach us and if we agree with their teachings then use it otherwise just move on there are many things around us which can provide us inspiration and guidance why to insist or depend on just one source.

The Power of Mother Sita in Modern World

Many people in India find it difficult to justify or reconcile themselves to the fact that in a culture which worships Saraswati as the Goddess of Learning, so many girls are deprived of even primary education; in a culture which worships Lakshmi as the Goddess of Wealth, so many modern-day Lakshmis live a slavish life of economic dependence; in a culture where male Gods have had to appeal for perfection to the feminine Shakti, women among many communities are not allowed to venture out of their domestic confines without male protection. This bewilderment and guilt has compelled numerous people to pick up cudgels on behalf of women, throwing up important social movements. It is noteworthy that a majority of women's rights struggles and movements in modern India have been often initiated, led and sustained by men.

In the nineteenth century, considered by many as a period of severe erosion of women's rights in India, Vidyasagar in Bengal, Ranade and Phule in Maharashtra, Veerasalingam in Andhra, Lala Devraj in Punjab and a host of others committed their entire lives to the cause of women. In the writings of these social reformers, cutting across regional and caste boundaries, woman as the wronged *matri shakti*, is a recurring metaphor. A good part of their efforts went into convincing other men that Indian society could not make progress as long as their partners stayed oppressed, that the country's freedom could not be won as long as women were denied their rightful due in the family and in society. To women, their message was that they should recognise their own feminine shakti and become modern-day Durgas without, of course, losing Sita's nurturing qualities.

Sita is considered a very negative role model, the hallmark of wifely slavery for most of those who consider themselves progressives and feminists. Her suffering is seen as a product of masochism, lack of selfhood and supine surrender to patriarchy. Many Indian "modernists" see Sita as an adversary whose influence among people is to be countered. The association of the feminine with nurturing mother figures is seen as a patriarchal conspiracy to put women in restrictive and self-effacing roles.

Ramcharitra Manas Sita cannot be an icon of today's women. Today they face different challenges than Sita faced in times of Ramayan. She had difficulties in her life and fought her way out. There might be some similarities in certain situations but value system and society structure is totally different today. So may be Sita cannot provide all the motivation necessary for modern women to excel.

Needless to say, this projection is altogether contrary to the popular perception of Sita. The Ramayana tells the story of a whole spectrum of voluntary sacrifices and hardships endured by most of the main characters in their resolve to adhere to their *dharmic* codes. However, it is Sita's sacrifices, and the raw deal meted out to her, that loom much larger in the Indian consciousness than the hardships undergone by any of the other characters in the epic. Sita emerges as the final moral touchstone of the story. Her pain and sorrow hang heavily on the collective consciousness of the Indian people like that of no other character, divine or mortal.

The popular obsession with Sita's predicament is rooted in the three episodes after her liberation from Ravana's captivity: her *agni pariksha* (ordeal by fire), her later banishment by Rama and, in the end, Rama's demand for a second fire-ordeal, which she rejects through an appeal to her mother, Prithvi (Goddess Earth), to receive her back into Her womb. These episodes, as depicted in the Valmiki Ramayana, have disturbed devotees and non-devotees alike throughout the centuries. Rama's treatment of Sita, in the latter parts of the Ramayana, remains immensely controversial and has provoked innumerable attempts by successive generations to critique and rework their relationship. From Kalidasa and Bhavabhuti to Kamban, Tulsidas and contemporary writers such as Bharat Bhushan Agarwal and Maithili Sharan Gupta, authors have challenged Rama's behavior towards Sita or have attempted to reform Rama to make him prove himself a more worthy husband for her.

This obsession with reforming Rama has to do with the popular perception of Sita as perfection incarnate, so much so that even *Maryada Purushottam* Rama, the Divinely Perfect Rama, does not measure up to her. Sita is seen as flawless, despite the fact that she brings about trouble for everyone by crossing the magic circle of protection around her forest hut. In this projection, people have voluntarily glossed over those few occasions when Sita behaves unreasonably as in her castigation of Lakshmana, accusing him of lustful intentions towards her at the time he refuses to follow her dictates and go to help Rama in the forest.

Whereas feminists interpret Sita's offer to undergo *agni pariksha* as an act of surrender to the whims of an unreasonable husband, in popular perception it is seen as an act of defiance that challenges her husband's aspersions. Sita emerges as a woman that even Agni, the Fire God–who has the power to destroy everything He touches–does not dare harm.

While no one in India feels offended if Rama is asked to improve, reform and change some of his anti-women notions, people unencumbered by "isms" are not enthusiastic about Sita being subjected to "improvements" which make her behave altogether out of character. Politically inspired attempts to make Sita lose the very qualities that make her Sita are resented or simply dismissed by those who have some roots in their culture and tradition.

If we want people to gracefully yield space for our newly acquired ideologies, we have to learn to be tolerant and respectful of those they already hold. There is no need to treat our traditional Gods and Goddesses as adversaries, especially considering that they are willing to come a long way to support our causes. At the heart of this controversy between these two opposing approaches to social and religious reform is the key question: How do we relate to our cultural heritage and define our relationship to our own people and the values they cherish?

Do we disown tradition and position ourselves outside it, or do we accept it as our own, in the way we accept our gene stock? Owning up to our traditions does not imply subscribing to every one of their pathological norms and endorsing harmful practices. It simply means learning to distinguish between inherently unjust practices and those that one doesn't like because one has adopted a different value framework.

Social reformers can be effective only when people see them as caring insiders who have stood by them in their various trials and tribulations. But if we descend as attacking outsiders, focusing solely on practices we disapprove of, we will not make much of a dent. Only by creating a shared sense of right and wrong with the people whose lives we wish to change for the better can we create a new social consensus for a more just and humane society within our respective communities.

Mahatma Gandhi was among the most creative reformers who instinctively understood the creative potential of many of our traditions and values. For example, he used the Sita symbol to advocate the idea of women's strength, autonomy and ability to protect themselves rather than depend on men for safety. His Sita was like a "lioness in spirit" before which Ravana became "as helpless as a goat." For the protection of her virtues even in Ravana's custody, she did not "need the assistance of Rama." Her own purity was her sole shield.

Gandhi's Sita became a symbol of *swadeshi* or the decolonization of the Indian economy. He asked the women of India to follow her example by wearing Indian homespun and boycotting foreign fineries because Gandhi's Sita would have never worn imported fabric. Gandhi wanted to create a whole army of new Sitas who were not brought up to think that a woman "was well only with her husband or on the funeral pyre." He wanted them to stop aspiring to be mere wives and instead become leaders of men, teaching them the message of peace and social harmony.

Even those who are put off by Gandhi's use of Hindu religious symbols for political mobilization and who have problems with many of his views on women and sexuality do not deny that, more than any other modern leader, he helped create a favorable atmosphere for women's large scale and respectful entry into public life. Gandhi's moral backing legitimized women's right to hold political office without having to wage long-drawn battles, like the Suffragists in the West had to do to. His Sitas were encouraged to break the shackles of domesticity, to come out of purdah, to lead political movements and teach the art of peace to this warring world.

House wives pertain as early as five in the morning to late at night: feeding the cattle, followed by all the chores required for the upkeep of the house and its surroundings, cooking, fetching water, and the care of children. All these by themselves represent a full day's work. But she goes on non-stop.

"After completing housework, she goes to the fields and, at the end of a back-breaking day of work, on her way back home, she tries to scrounge around and collect anything that can be used as firewood for the evening meal. Then she follows with a second round of tasks–cooking the evening meal, looking after little children, feeding the animals and tending to the needs of other family members including the old and sick. From the time she wakes up to feed the cattle to the time she lays down to sleep, she has probably put in no less than 15 hours of work. How do you calculate in rupee terms the love, care and affection that she puts into all these tasks? How do you put a money value on the services of a person who saves the honor of the family by going and stealthily borrowing milk or sugar from the neighbors so she can provide tea for your guests who come at an unexpected hour at a time when the house does not have those provisions? Let us put the value of all these acts of loyalty and love at zero. But shouldn't she get at least as much money as a person working for the Employment Guarantee Scheme gets for simply moving earth from one place to another?"

"Let us figure out the value of her labor on the basis of a minimum wage of 120 rupees per day [US $2]. She works 365 days a year. Let us say she has been married to you for 20 years. Given that she has worked 365 days a year for 20 years, the amount comes to more than 8,76,000 rupees [$ 14,600]. She has never tried to demand this amount you owe her, nor sent a notice with a jeep load of people to come, seize and take away your household utensils as the bank officials do when you owe much smaller amounts as agricultural loans to government banks. On the contrary, to save you from other creditors, remember how often she even sold off the little bit of jewellery she was wearing? If we calculate the total, along with the interest, it comes to a minimum of 39,60,000 rupees [$ 66,000]. What have you given her in return?

Two saris for a whole year and that, too, forgotten if there is a drought. No guarantee of even adequate food. If there is not enough food in the house, the husband's share is not reduced. And a mother will hardly snatch food away from her own children's mouths. She makes do with whatever is left over–a half or a quarter chapati and fills the rest of her stomach by drinking water. This has been her fate so far."

Having thus established the credentials of their wives as no less self-effacing than Sita Mata herself, that they are emulating a very negative role model and being as ungrateful and uncaring as was Rama:

"That this situation is not new is certain. But how and when did it start? *Prabhu* Ramchandra is considered a *purushottam*, the ideal human. But think of how he treated Sita Mata, who joyfully embraced exile in the forest for 14 years to be with him. As soon as Rama was appointed as king, he decided to cast her off. It is not necessary for us to get into a debate on whether it was right or not for Rama to give up Sita. But was it not necessary for him to at least take the trouble of explaining to Sita why, as a king, he was compelled to abandon her? He could have assured her that she need not lack anything after his parting company with her, that she could continue living respectably in Ayodhya. Better still, Rama should have told his subjects: 'If she is not good enough for you as a queen, I will go along with her.' After all that is what she had done when Rama was banished by Kaikeyi who had told Sita she could continue living in the palace. But Sita had said, '*Jithe Rama, tithe Sita*'; ["Wherever Ram goes, there goes Sita"]. Even if Rama was not ready to leave his kingship for her, surely there were less cruel ways to deal with the situation. Sita was pregnant at that time. If Rama had provided her a small straw hut till the time of her delivery, he would not have lost any of his greatness by doing so."

Link the story to an architectural relic which stands as testimony to the injustice done to Sita in popular imagination: "There is a Sita temple at Raveri village of Maharashtra. The villagers in that area tell you that Sita Mata delivered her two sons on that very spot. She was in such a destitute condition that she went begging for a handful of grains. The people of village Raveri spurned her and refused to give her any. Sita Mata cursed them in her grief. Such was the power of that curse that not a grain of wheat would grow in that village for centuries (until the arrival of the hybrid variety), even though the neighboring villages produced plentiful harvests of wheat. In other words, the poverty of Indian farmers will not go away unless they get rid of the curse of Mother Sita by atoning for the misdeed of Rama. They can do so by repaying their debt to their own Lakshmis and free themselves of her curses. After all the husband of a slave cannot be a free man.

No modern-day Sita would ever have to suffer the fate of Rama's Sita because she had nothing to call her own, no house or property of her own. By transferring land to their wives, they were paying off "a long overdue debt" to Mother Sita: Through this gesture, farmer will be vanquishing that monster of male tyranny which even Prabhu Ram could not vanquish though he slayed a greater warrior like Ravana with ease.

For as long as it lasted, this unique campaign was able to draw deep emotional response because Mother Sita has the power to guilt-trip the most hard-hearted Hindu men to respond to her plea for justice. Needless to say, this campaign for women's economic rights could take off in rural Maharashtra in large part due to Joshi's charisma and credibility as a leader.

Sita: The Original Iron Lady

Right from childhood every girl child in Indian family trained and tutored to view Sita with tremendous compassion, extreme reverence and even pity. Over the centuries, this is how she has been viewed. Tears and Sita have been inseparable. Talking about her, singing her tale, thinking about her, people usually have wet eyes. One doesn't have to go far to testify the truth of matter. '*Ramayana Paath*' is a very common practice in the northern part of our country. Child birth, marriages, house warming ceremonies, any auspicious happening is reason enough for people to call a '*mandali*' and the '*paath*' starts. Every mention of Sita is coupled with blocked throats and wet eyes. This response to Sita is infectious. It has been passed to us over the centuries. It's in our DNA.

To imagine that any piece of writing would be able to change all this would be foolish indeed. Strange as it may sound. there's nothing exactly pitiable about this woman. Sita does not deserve our pity. This kind of a response might be a way of escaping the real issues. It might be something else. But Sita should arouse our admiration, awe, respect, love but certainly not pity.

It's worth noting at this point that people in India don't name their daughters after Sita. She is worshipped but from afar; she's not brought near in the form of daughters, sisters, wives, neighbors and so on. Why they don't call their daughter Sita become she suffered a lot in this world, they don't name their daughters as Sita. They don't want their daughter to suffer like her. So seductresses like Urvashi and Menaka would do but not a woman like Sita who stood up for her dignity and successfully stood her ground.

This is a telling tale on Indian mind-set. We don't accept strong woman. Pleading women, weeping women, seducing women, foolish women, superficial women - you name any brand and we accept them. But we don't accept strong women. Strength, mental superiority and iron-ness are things we don't savor in our women. A woman who can control her instincts is a potential threat to male superiority and status quo. Deep down, the male mind fears a woman who does not fall a prey to her instincts. No temptation comes from outside. The enemy lies within us. A woman can be carried away '*samundar paar*', can be ill treated, all time tested mechanisms, '*Sam, dam, bhaya, bhed*' can be applied on her; yet she can stand her ground. She can do it with a barrier of a grass blade because walls and veils do not protect a woman's dignity; her mind does. Mental strength is the only strength.

Ravana says that he is young, handsome, wealthy, powerful and attractive; Sita is a bundle of bewitchment; together they'd walk on the ocean beach. She'd be adorned with the best jewels in the world. Her father's family would be rewarded with wealth. Hundreds of maids would look after her day and night.

Ravana at this point is the personification of '*aasakti*' (indulgence of senses). Valmiki's description is highly suggestive. Wine, woman, disarranged clothes, and entangled jewels and clothes–all present the heady picture of enjoyment of senses. Ravana is in the celebration of senses. Sita is in the celebration of the soul. He's looking outside; she's looking within herself. Here's a young, beautiful princess, recently married to a very lovable prince. She's on her honeymoon. Brutally broken from her lover, who's her husband, she's asked to submit to another man. Obviously she's being treated as a commodity. Her feelings do not matter for the man who wants to ravish her as a dish on his much stuffed platter. The will of the male is considered to be supreme. She reverses the order; her will prevails. The male will is defeated. There can be no stronger feminist symbol than Sita.

Sita, if we look independently is the original '*satya-agrahi*'. Forced to live in Lanka, she refuses to take food, to dress up, in short, to enjoy life. Her mourning becomes her being. She's seduced. She's tortured. She's shown fear. The '*raakshasis*' around her are instructed to mould her in whatever manner they can. The flame of her pure heart converts people like Trijata even in the land of demons.

An epic scene from an immortal epic. The two flows of life - '*tamsik*' (consumption based) and '*satwik*' (abstinence based) are there for everyone to see. The presentation is powerful. Sita is slim. She's beautiful. She's vulnerable or so she seems to be. She's lonely. She's deep in sorrow. Ravana, on the other hand is the king. He's in his own territory. He's powerful or so he seems to be. He's deep in erotic pleasures of life. To top it all, he's brought Sita to Lanka. He's relishing the prospect of enjoying her. Here's a complete contrast. No worldly wisdom can predict that Sita would win and Ravana would lose.

Sita challenges the basic patriarchal mind-set which treats women as pawn for all sorts of reasons – revenge, insult, scoring points, conveying messages, fulfilling long nurtured complexes and so on. There can be more reasons. Why do we have all solid abuses in our country based on women? 'Your mother', 'your sister' – we all know them only too well. Women are symbols of weakness. Only women have honor; men do not share such useless things.

Ravana was also fulfilling his long cherished complex. He was rejected by Sita in her '*swayambar*' – this might be the reason. His sister was insulted by the brothers, Ram and Laxman – that might be the reason. But his wrath had to fall on a lonely, simple, unarmed, unprotected woman. Sita refuses to pay the price. She refuses to become a prey of his complicated complexes. She reverts the cycle.

Her commitment is first and foremost to her own self. Her confidence and dedication emanate from her self-respect. She is fighting for her own, personal, individual dignity; more than for anything else. She's reversing the canon that fathers, husbands and sons are the keepers of women; women have to follow the dictates of one of the three categories of men throughout their lives. She crosses the *Laxman Rekha* only moments after it is made. Plunged into calamity, she's her own keeper. Her actions say that a woman will decide her own destiny. The will of the woman will matter. No one can force a woman into any act.

The only strange thing in her case is that usually freedom means promiscuity; she has chosen the path less traveled. Sita says that freedom means to go for more than one partner or not to go for more than one partner. Freedom does not necessarily mean getting wild. This is a unique correction on our generally conceived idea of freedom. You ask anyone about the freedom of a married woman and without wasting a second; images of infidelity would start dancing before the eyes. We have simply not thought about the freedom to say 'no'. This is the greatest form of freedom. When you say 'no', you're definitely spelling a specific choice, 'I want this and not this'. Here's freedom coupled with discretion and decision.

The definition of freedom is not limited to getting wild. If I have the freedom to violate norms, I must also have the freedom to follow the norms. I just cannot accept the slavery of 'getting wild'. Getting into newer chains and often dirtier, is not freedom. Freedom is free application of mind. In this context, Sita's mental strength is admirable. Freedom to say 'no' to patterns of behavior your rational mind does not approve of; this.

Sita is in the habit of taking her own decisions. Her words and actions propel the epic. Not only does she take a stand on her choice of a partner, she sets the agenda for Ram. She's very specific. She spells the exact time limit within which Ram has to come and perform the most important part of his '*leela*' on earth – public killing of Ravana. Hanuman clearly says that he can carry her back easily but her response is laden with sound reasons – Hanuman's safety, her own safety, her married status and above everything else resurrection of the stature of Ram. Ram should act only the way that befits him. There's no other way but public killing of Ravana by Ram. Sita spells the details, the lines which everyone has to follow. Sita's message is clear. She is not for the short cut. Being born in this less than perfect world, there's no point in being afraid of miseries or hardships. What matters is the way one deals with challenges. That is the most important thing.

Let one showed to take away all the weeping associated with Sita in our country. Perhaps it is good for our own catharsis. It cleanses us of many dark and hidden fears. But this lady is a fighter, a truly strong person. Sita and Ram are imbedded in the collective consciousness of our country. What must have started with a young prince killing an evil king has now become the reservoir of all that we wish to see in ourselves. Ram is truth. Ram is righteousness. Ram is beautiful. Sita is purity. Sita is goodness. Sita is strength. Sita is the original iron lady.

Sita is a Iron Lady .. not alone a Iron Lady .. she is an Iron Lady (soft Iron lady) the Ramayana is written not as a story of individual it is the style of life and all the character in Ramayana are unique in its role and all are great rolls even the Frontline Monkeys is an model role and we should learn how they are unite and building the *(Sethu)* bridge to enable Rama to reach Lanka. Remember the monkeys not having the sixth sense and not expected any return and just want to help others.

Ravana is not a Bad character it is an character which say how he respect the feeling of his sister and I will say the real good nature of Rama, Laxmana, Sita or Hanuman came out only because of this Acts and behaviour.

Sita did not actually reverse any patriarchal mindset or practice, she reinforced them. Most of her actions consistent with the most traditional and conservative thought. Just putting up a bunch of random arbitrary conditions for Ram does not make her an iron lady, it makes her the storyteller's pawn, a nice explanation for an unnecessary battle. And it makes her suffer unnecessarily. Freedom usually means going wild because traditional wisdom says not to go wild. If you are completely independent and free, what's the use if you don't defy some of the rules that everyone else follows? You might as well remain "un-free", it's not like it's going to make any difference! As far as I can tell, Sita never defied any traditions or beliefs, even those which are obviously unfair towards women.

All this behavior shows us that Sita was a woman who got caught up in the middle, and suffered.

I am obliged and indebted to my department and senior officers and colleagues who have provided necessary help and guidance in writing this book. I am very much indebted to Justice R.B. Dixit (Retd.) for his constant guidance and help in writing this book. I am obliged to all the writers of the book which I have consulted in writing this book. I am also thankful to Originals (an imprint of Low Price Publications) who has agreed to publish this book. The help extended by M/s Gupta Services, Gwalior in typing of this book cannot be forgotten.

I owe a deep debt to my family members for their reverential and encouraging attitude. I would not have found a congenial environment at home for under taking the onerous task of writing a book in difficult times, covering a wide range of complex issues of feminism.

I shall welcome criticism and suggestions for further improving the quality of this book from readers and critics.

Gwalior
Thakur Shailendra Nath

Ph. 07697014309, 09826085246

e-mail thakurshailendranath@yahoo.com.

1

Shakti

Shakti, meaning sacred force or empowerment, is the primordial cosmic energy and represents the dynamic forces that are thought to move through the entire universe. Shakti is the concept, or personification, of divine feminine creative power, sometimes referred to as 'The Great Divine Mother'. On the earthly plane, Shakti most actively manifests through female embodiment and creativity/fertility, though it is also present in males in its potential, unmanifest form.

Not only is the Shakti responsible for creation, it is also the agent of all change. Shakti is cosmic existence as well as liberation, its most significant form being the *Kundalini Shakti*, a mysterious psycho-spiritual force. Shakti exists in a state of *svâtantrya*, dependence on no-one, being interdependent with the entire universe.

Shakti is worshipped as the Supreme Being. However, in other Hindu traditions of Shaivism and Vaishnavism, Shakti embodies the active feminine energy *Prakriti* of *Purusha*, who is Vishnu in Vaishnavism or Shiva in Shaivism. Vishnu's female counterpart is called Lakshmi, with Parvati being the female half of Shiva.

The beginning of Creation, as it is written in the Shakta Advaita, the Divine Mother took form and set in motion the wheel of manifestation. She bestowed her healing spirit into the womb and regenerative energy of every female of every species of the earth. According to the Vedas (as written or sung by the rishika), a woman's femininity cannot exist apart from her Shakti, and Shakti is a metaphor for womanhood.

David Kinsley believes that the concept of "Shakti" may be derived from Lord Indra's consort Sachi (Indrani), meaning power. Indrani is part of a group of seven or eight mother goddesses called the Matrikas (Brahmani, Vaishnavi, Maheshvari, Indrani, Kumari, Varahi and Chamunda and/or Narasimhi), who are considered Shaktis of major Hindu gods (Brahma, Vishnu, Shiva, Indra, Skanda, Varaha/Yama, Devi and Narasimha respectively).

Lakshmi

Lakshmi is the Hindu goddess of wealth, prosperity (both material and spiritual), fortune, and the embodiment of beauty. She is the consort of the god Vishnu. Also called Mahalakshmi, she is said to bring good luck and is believed to protect her devotees from all kinds of misery and money-related sorrows. Lakshmi is called *Shri* or *Thirumagal* because she is endowed with six auspicious and divine qualities, or *Gunas*, and also because she is the source of strength even to Vishnu. When Vishnu incarnated on earth as avatars Rama and Krishna, Lakshmi incarnated as his consort. Sita (Rama's wife), Radha (Krishna's lover) and Rukmini and the other wives of Krishna are considered forms of Lakshmi.

Evolution and Legends

Devas (gods) and *Asuras* (demons) were both mortal at one time. *Amrit*, the divine nectar that would grant immortality, could be obtained only by churning the *Kshirsagar* (Ocean of Milk). The *devas* and *asuras* both sought immortality and decided to churn the *Kshirsagar*. With the *devas* on one side and the *asuras* on the other, the *samudra manthan* commenced. Vishnu incarnated as Kurma, the tortoise, on whom was placed a mountain as a churning pole; Vasuki, the great venom-spewing serpent, was wrapped around it and used to churn the ocean. A host of divine celestial objects came up during the churning. Among these, was the goddess Lakshmi, the daughter of the king of the milky ocean (Varuna). Some tells daughter of Kuber. The last to come up was the *amrita*. With this, the avatar of Kurma, the tortoise, ended. Vishnu then took up the form of a beautiful maiden to distract the *asuras* and gave immortality to the *devas*. In Mahalakshmi story, she is *shakti roopa* of *parabrahma* or *adi dev narayan*.

Mahalakshmi has always existed. Her appearance from *samudra manthan* is her main manifestation only. Mahalakshmi was also born to the great sage Bhrigu, and she is therefore also called Bhargavi. Mahalakshmi is also the sister of the great guru Sukracharya as well as the great planet Chandra. Each time Vishnu descends on earth as an *avatar*, He is accompanied by an *avatar* of Lakshmi.

The moon (*chandra*) also appeared from the ocean during the churning, making it her brother. Alakshmi, the goddess of misfortune, is Lakshmi's elder sister. According to the Vishnu Purana, Lakshmi is the daughter of Bhrigu and Khyaati and resided in *Swarga*, but, due to the curse of Durvasa, she left *Swarga* and made *Kshirsagara* her home.

The etymology and meanings of the word Lakshmi is given in Monier Williams' Sanskrit–English Dictionary compiled in the 19th century in British India.

1. Laksmika meaning a mark, sign, or token is in Rig Veda, 71, 2 and Nirukta iv, 10.
2. Laksmi (with or without *papi*) is a bad sign or an impending misfortune referred to Atharva Veda and Apasthambha Shrauta Sutra.
3. In older Sanskrit, it is usually used with "*punya*" meaning a good sign, good fortune, prosperity, success, or happiness in Atharva Veda.
4. Laksmi personifies wealth, riches, beauty, loveliness, grace, charm and splendour in Mahabharata.
5. Laksmi as a noun is a goddess of fortune and beauty (frequently in the later mythology identified with Sri and regarded as the wife of Visnu or Narayana).
6. According to Sir Monier Williams, "Religious thought and life in India", 45, 40-43 she sprang with other precious things from the foam of the ocean when churned by the gods and demons for the recovery of the *Amrita.* She appeared with a lotus in her hand, whence she is also called Padma.
7. According to another legend, she appeared at the creation floating over the water on the expanded petals of a lotus flower; she is

also variously regarded as wife of Surya, as wife of Praja-pati, as wife of Dharma and mother of Kama, as sister or mother of Dhat[and Vidhat[, as wife of Dattatreya, as one of the nine Saktis of Visnu, as a manifestation of Prakrti, as identified with Dakshayani in Bharatasrama, and with Sita, wife of Rama, and with other women.

Mahalakshmi is the presiding Goddess of the Middle episode of Devi Mahatmya. Here, she is depicted as Devi in her universal form as Shakti. The manifestation of the Devi to kill Mahishasura is formed by the effulgences of all the gods. The Goddess is described as eighteen-armed, bearing a string of beads, battle axe, mace, arrow, thunderbolt, lotus, bow, water pot, cudgel, lance, sword, shield, conch, bell, wine cup, trident, noose and the disc "*sudarsana*". She has a complexion of coral and is seated on a lotus. She is known as Ashta Dasa Bhuja Mahalakshmi.

She is seen in two forms, Bhudevi and Sridevi, both either side of Sri Venkateshwara or Vishnu. Bhudevi is the representation and totality of the material world or energy, called the aparam Prakriti, in which she is called Mother Earth. Sridevi is the spiritual world or energy, called the Prakriti. Most people are mistaken that they are separate beings although they are one, Lakshmi. Lakshmi is the power of Lord Vishnu.

Mahalakshmi's presence is also found on Lord Sri Venkateswara (at Tirumala) or Vishnu's chest, at the heart. Lakshmi is the embodiment of love, from which devotion to God or Bhakti flows from. It is through Love/Bhakti or Lakshmi that the *atma* or soul is able to reach God or Vishnu. Lakshmi plays a special role as the mediator between her husband Lord Vishnu and His worldly devotees. While Vishnu is often conceived of as a stern, easily perturbed patriarch, Lakshmi represents a more soothing, warm and approachable mother figure who willingly intervenes in the lives of devotees on His behalf. Often, it is Lakshmi who acts as the advocate for the request of a given mortal. When asking Vishnu for grace or the forgiveness of sins, Hindus often approach Him through the intermediary presence of Lakshmi. She is also the personification of the spiritual Fulfillment. Also, she embodies the spiritual world, also known as Vaikunta, the abode of Lakshmi-Narayana or Vishnu, or what would be considered Heaven in Vaishnavism. She is also the divine qualities of God and the soul. Lakshmi is the embodiment of God's superior spiritual feminine energy, or one of main forms of Adi Parashakti, Param Prakriti, which purifies, empowers and uplifts the individual. Hence, she is called the Goddess of Fortune. Due to her motherly feelings and being the consort of Narayan (Supreme Being), she is believed as the Mother of the Universe.

In India common titles standing in for the English Mr. & Mrs. are Shri and Shrimati. The prefix "shri " translates as "One who takes delight in" Anything that need be affluent gets the auspicious prefix and suffix 'Shri' or 'Lakshmi'.

Philosophy

Devi Mahatmya accepts the ancient Vedic tradition in the form of Vâk and Trayî Vidyâ and the philosophical doctrine of the codified system of Samkhya (Prakriti manifesting as the three Gunas) and Vedânta as Paramavidyâ, the cause of Mukti. Further it synthesizes the then prevailing local Mother goddess cults of Aryan and non-Aryan origin.

It is said "all lives are conscious, but that knowledge is connected with senses. That goddess Bhagavatî, granting all kinds of prosperity, makes even the wise attracted to worldly pleasures and things forcibly with her great power of attraction. This ever-changing world with all its animate and inanimate things, is created by her. As the cause of salvation she turns into supreme spiritual knowledge, and is thus eternal; and again as the cause of bondage to worldly things she turns into things mundane and is the mistress of all, including Gods. She is eternal (and is thus beyond our knowledge) and pervades the world which may accordingly be called her form. Yet for the assistance of the lustrous souls, she appears in different forms."

The framing narrative of Devi Mahatmya presents a dispossessed king, a merchant betrayed by his family, and a sage whose teachings lead them both beyond existential suffering. The sage instructs by recounting three different epic battles between the Devi and various demonic adversaries (the three tales being governed respectively by, Mahakali (Chapter 1), Mahalakshmi (Chapters 2-4) and Mahasaraswati (Chapters 5-13) . Most famous is the story of Mahishasura Mardini – Devi as "Slayer of the Buffalo Demon" – one of the most ubiquitous images in Hindu art and sculpture, and a tale known almost universally in India. Among the important goddess forms the Devi Mahatmyam introduced into the Sanskritic mainstream are Kali and the Sapta-Matrika ("Seven Mothers").

Thus both he and I, drawn by attachment towards objects whose defects we do know, are exceedingly unhappy. How does this happen, then, sir, that though we are aware of it, this delusion persists? This delusion besets me as well as him, blinded as we are in respect of discrimination?

Every being has the knowledge of objects perceivable by the senses. And object of sense reaches it in various ways. Some beings are blind by day, and others are blind by night; some beings have equal sight both by day and night. Human beings are certainly endowed with knowledge, but they are not the only beings (to be so endowed), for cattle, birds, animals and other creatures also cognise (objects of senses).

The knowledge that men have, birds and beasts too have; and what they have men also possess; and the rest (like eating and sleeping) is common to both of them. Look at these birds, which though they possess knowledge, and are themselves distressed by hunger are yet, because of the delusion, engaged in feeding grains into the beaks of their young ones. See with what devotion they put the food grains into the beaks of their young ones? Men, O king, are full of desires. Human beings are, O tiger among men, attached to their children because of greed, expecting rewards in return.

Even so men are hurled into the whirlpool of attachment, the pit of delusion, through the power of Mahamaya (the Great delusion), who makes the existence of the world possible. Marvel not at this. This Mahamaya is the Yoganidra, of Vishnu, the Lord of the world. It is by her the world is deluded. Verily she, the Bhagavati, the Mahamaya forcibly drawing the minds of even the wise, entangles them into delusion. She creates this entire universe, both moving and unmoving. It is she who, when propitious, becomes a boon-giver to human beings for their final liberation. She is the supreme knowledge, the cause of final liberation, and eternal; she is the cause of the bondage of transmigration and the sovereign over all lords.

The Rishi said:

Mahamaya Devi is eternal, embodied as the universe. By her all this is pervaded. Nevertheless she incarnates in manifold ways; hear it from me. When she manifests herself in order to accomplish the purposes of the *devas*, she is said to be born in the world, though she is eternal.

The Devisukta (RV 10.125) declares that the Goddess is the power expressed through all the gods, that they are united in her who shines with consciousness, that her presence is all-pervading, that she supports all of creation, that she is the source of righteousness and the revealer of truth, that she is the source of all worlds, yet that she shines transcendent beyond them.

Sakti, Suffering, and Power

Hindu culture conceives of self-sacrifice as a form of power. The submissive feminine role has more complexity than in the West. In fact, according to Margaret Egnor, a special, positive power comes from suffering. The goddess Sakti embodies this power; action of this sort is considered inherently female.

To begin with, sakti, like our word "power" is often defined as the ability to act, to make others act, to make things happen, and as action itself. . . . In as much as spiritual power of sakti is believed to be acquired through suffering, especially the suffering of servitude, one apparent contradiction is resolved: if women have more sakti than men, this is (at least in part) because women stand in the position of servants with respect to men. This also helps to explain why women, rather than trying to undo the sexual hierarchy, are often its staunchest supporters.

Egnor sees elements of choice and pride in women's emulation of the Sita-Savitri image. Whereas the women whose stories she presents obviously did not enjoy suffering, they did not see themselves as victims but rather women with sakti: "None of these women saw a contradiction between her possession of sakti and her subordinate role as female. . . . On the contrary, for each woman the possession of extraordinary sakti came as a consequence of her subordinate status, or more accurately, as a consequence of the suffering that that subordination entailed". Such a complex concept of suffering and spiritual power explains better why the Sita-Savitri image has persisted in literature until recently, when women writers affected by Western feminism have explored the alternative ideal of self-assertion.

Hindu culture's construction of suffering and giving makes clear how in Nectar in a Siege Rukmani's daughter could prostitute herself yet uphold the feminine ideal. Ira finds the power to defy her father and social norms, only because she acts out of self sacrifice: she goes out to make some money so that she can feed her dying brother during a famine. Her selling of her body does not violate the ideal of wifely loyalty and virtue, since her husband had divorced her for not bearing children. Yet again, as in the case of Rukmani's enraged rebellion against a tomentor, Markandya punishes the suffering woman's defiance and makes it futile. With the cruel irony of the story Ira's brother dies despite her attempts, and she finally becomes pregnant from one of her customers, bearing an defective-looking child who increases her shame. Yet she cares for him with love and accepts him as she would a child born to happier circumstances. Just like her mother, no end comes to her endurance and caring for others in her family.

2

Mithila

During his tour to Mithila to participate in the *Dhanuryagya* organised by the King Janaka for marriage of his daughter Sita, Rama had finished journey between the river Son and the Ganges before reaching Vaishali within a day only. It took Visvamitra along with Rama and Lakshmana, four days to reach the capital of the country of Videha from Ayodhya. They rested on the way for one night only.

Mithila is the name of the land situated between 25°28' and 26°52' N latitude and between 84°56' and 86°46' E bounded on the north by the Himalayas (Nepal) on the east by the Mahananda (the river Kosi has shifted 130 km west) on the south by the river Ganga and on west by the river Gandaki (earlier known as Sadanira). From the foot hills of the Himalayas in the north to the Ganga in the south it stretches for more than 170 km and from the Mahananda in the east to the river Gandaki in the west, it stretches to 425 km. It is remarkable that it has rivers on three sides and the Himalayas on one.

Mithila was consistently regarded as an independent unit of the Prayagadesa. Praci, an ancient Tibetan works, excluded even Magadha, Kasi and Kosala but included Mithila and Vanga. Only in Brihad Vishnu Purana (5th cen. A.D)., Mithila Mahatmaya II Khamla Tirabhukti (a later name of the province) Mithila is described as situated between the river Ganga and the Himalayas, extending over fifteen rivers and from Kosi (Kausiki, in the east) to the Gandaki in the west, for 24 *yojanas* and from Ganga to the forests of Himalayas for 16 *Yojanas*. The messengers sent by Janaka reached Dasaratha's capital in three days by travelling very fast, while Dasaratha on his journey to the Videhan capital in his chariot took four days.

At first it seems that the whole province was called Videha and had several kingdoms in it, the chief ones being those of Mithila and Vaisali. Indeed, from the account in earlier literature it would seem that the chief city of the kingdom of Mithila, was Mithila. The name Videha appears to have lost vogue in the mediaeval times. Then came the name Tirabhukti 4th and 5th centuries A.D. The Basarh terracotta seals of the 4th century A.D. mention this name for the first time. It became very popular and its simplified form, Tirhut, is now used extensively, though, the name Mithila is now gradually gaining ground. 'Tirhut' also indicated at one time a Sirkar (a division of the Subah of Bihar) under Muslim rulers ; it comprised of a very large tract of Brilhad-Vishnu Purana Mithilakhanda : Milimla; Tirabhukti; Vaidehi; Naimikanarn the forest associated with the descendants of Nimi; Jnanakehelram, Kripa-pitham-the home of knowledge and the centre of grace; Svarnalangalpaddhari-The footsteps of the gold plough; Janakijanmabhumi; Vihalmashn-Devoid of sins ; Ramanandakuri-the cottage of Sita's Pleasure; Visvahharani-world pleasant; and Nityamangala-ever blissful.

Britishers formed the modern division of Tirhut comprising the Districts of Muzaffarpur, Darbhanga, Champaran and Saran. 'Videha' is the earliest designation, probably derived from the name of the Vedic King Videgha Mathava who is said to have introduced the Agni into the lands beyond the river Sadanira. Visit led to the cultivation and more habitation of the country, for we are told that previously the land was extremely marshy and had to he dried. Mithila is not mentioned in the Vaidika or post-Vaidika Literature. It is used most extensively in literature especially as the capital city of Videha or Tirabhukti province situated somewhere in the Tarai–modern Janakpur. Mithila is also called Miyulu in the Buddhist Annals. The origin of the name Mithila too in the title Mathava king, Mithi being reminiscent of it. In some Jataka accounts a city called Jayanta on the bank of the Gangas is spoken of as the capital of Videha. The Devi Bhogarata (*Skandhe* 6) wrongly located the city on the bank of the Ganga. The use of the appellation 'Mithila' along with 'Tirabhukti' or Tirhut for the whole country is comparatively very late-from about the time of the installation of Karnata Dynasty in 1097 A.D.

The Valmikiya Ramayana observes that the city of Mithila was founded by king Mithi. The most reasonable explanation of the origin of the name appears to be as given by the Unadi-sutras. Its authors derives it from '*manthan*' (to churn), name of the capital city came to be used for the whole kingdom. Tirabhukti is so called because it is regard as a land of three mythical sacrifices performed at the birth place of Sita, it extends up to the Tira or the bank of the Ganga, so it is called Tirabhuhti, two sides of the river Kausiki (the Kosi). This area is even today divided into two broad groups: Pachharari and Purvaripara. The extent of Mithila as given in the Brihad-Vishnu Purana, are East to West 96 *Kosas* or 24 *Yojanas*, North to South 64 *Kosas* or 16 *Yojanas*. Aha-janaha Jataka as 300 *Yojanas* and about 10000 sq miles in the kingdoms of Nepal. According to the Bhavishya Purana Nimi the son of Manu, king of Ayodhya frequented the land of sacrifices. His son Mithi founded a kingdom here which was named Mithila after his name. Being a 'city builder', he came to be known as 'Janaka'.

Geology looks further than history, scholars who have engaged themselves in the study of Ancient India have complete ignored Pre-historic Mithila, watery nature of its land particularly because of its situation at the foot of the Himalayas and by the frequent changes in the courses of its numerous rivers and rivulets have made it difficult to collect materials in the field of pre-historic antiquities. Marshy character of the land, Jalodbhara i.e. reclaimed from swamp. It was cultivated by the Brahmanas, who had caused agni, the Fire God, to taste it through sacrifices vast chain of temporary lakes, joined together by the numerous beds of hill streams of Nepal to the Ganges. Communications are open for only three or four months of the year. The river side is so common that the expression 'aadi dim' is used by everyone irrespective of age for going out for excreting. Wild animals used to roam about till recently, the long grass which grows in abundance in such a land, all these give the picture of Mithila gradually coming out of water in the Cain-Ozoic Epoch. The story of the Avatiras is believed by a group of scholars to indicate the gradual stages of evolution, especially that of Vishnu as half-tortoise and half-fish. We have in Mithila, in the first instance the famous Varaha-kshetra Tirtha, which map indicate the evolution of man through the stage of a boar; and then there is a Pauranic story of the birth of Narakasura by the Union of Vishnu and Varaha. This may indicate in some form, the knowledge or existence of the evolution of the primitive man from half-animals and half-man in Mithila of the ages that followed the age of sub-men or primitive men, the remains are so scanty in India that much cannot be said about any region, especially that of Mithila, which has been so far practically remained wholly unexplored.

There is a great paucity of material to eliminate the 'Pre-Vedic' inhabitants of Mithila. The various types of skulls that were discovered at the site near Darbhanga Railway Station, which is called 'Harahi', (i.e. the site of bones), remained unclassified and unstudied. There is a pond there, in the name of 'Harahi'. All that is possible in the present state of our knowledge is to look forward to the study of some apparently primitive castes and tribes of Mithila. As early as the 5th century AD, several tribes made up the Vajjian Confederacy and one of the most important of them was 'Lichchhavis', who was held for a long time to be of foreign stock. The names of other important ones are mentioned in the Jyotirisvara's Varnaratnakara. They are Tatama, Dhanukha, Goara, Khatbe, Amata etc.

In the earlier part of Satapatha Brahmana it is mentioned that King Videh Mathawa carried Agni in his mouth and he moved from Saraswati, in the Punjab, where the king dwelt, to Sadanira, drying up all the rivers. He did not, however, burnt Sadanira. The Brahmanas did not cross it, therefore, thinking it has not been burnt over by Agni Vaisvanar. But when Mathawa reached the Sadanira, he asked the Agni where will be his dwelling and the reply was that he should live to the East of Sadanira. However, it is fact that Ayodhya and Videha were long united and their Kings were of the same tree. It might mean that the reformed Brahmanism passed from the Bharata Kingdom to Ayodhya and then to Videha. The Videha country received Vedic culture long before the trine of the compilation of this Brahamana. In Brihaddranyaka Upanishad which forms a part of the Satapatha Brahmana Samrat Janaka is mentioned as a great patron of Vedic culture and it is said that the Videha Brahmanas were superior to the Kuru Panchalas in the Upanishadic phase of the development of vedic culture. The vedic (Aryan) culture has taken its root long before the Brahmana age, most probably in the early Samhita age of the Rigveda.

The Yajurveda Samhita mentions the famous cows of Videha. The Vedic sites were unknown to the inhabitants of Mithila. Mathawa Videha's priest Gautama Rahugana is credited in the Satapatha Brahmana with the discovery of the Mitravinda sacrifice which is further said to have been revived by Emperor Janaka through Yajnaavalkya. Besides, earlier still, Nami Sapya, King of Videha (Vaideha-Raja) is held up as a memorable example of a monarch who successfully performed elaborate sacrifices and thereby reached heaven. As the name of this King appears in several passages in the Rigveda, very early period in the development of Vedic Culture in India. Rig Veda 1.53.7 says that Nami was the friend and associate of Indra in quarelling the Asura Namuci, in the fight with Namuci, Indra protected Nami Sapya. The priest Gautama Rahugana is one of the important Rishi in Rigveda. It may be noted that the Brahmanic culture must have made a very rapid progress in the country to justify its description in the latter part of the Satapatha Brahmana as the centre of intellectual activity of the age. The Mahabharata attests that the Vedic lore was as popular in the East as anywhere else. In the Shanti Parva and in the Brihadaranyaka Upanishad, the authorship of Sukla Yajurveda is ascribed in clear terms to Yajnavalkya Vajasaneya, who belonged to Mithila.

From a perusal of all these things it becomes clear that Mithila figures prominently in ancient history from the very beginning of the Vedic period. Mithila was visited by Videgha Mathawa and his followers and probably, its marshes and jungles were cleared, and its soil was cultivated and a great and powerful kingdom was founded. Vedic Mithila knew other kings too, such as, Nami Sapya (Rigveda 1.53.7) and Par Ahlara. Nimi Vaideha, who is reported in certain Puranas to have founded this line of Kings in Mithila, is perhaps a later name of the king of Kings. At any rate, Videha Mathawa should be regarded as the earliest known King, if not the founder, of the Videha kingdom and of the line of Vaideha Janaka. In course of time it seems that a confederacy of kindered peoples known as the Kosala Videha, occupying a position no less important than that of the Kuru Panchalas, grow up at the time of the Redaction of the Brahmana. The Kingdom thus founded by the Vedic Mathawa was in course of time ruled by the Vedic *Samrat* Janaka the contemporary of Aruni and Yajnavalkya, and Ashvapati, a king of the Kekayas. Majajanaka II,12th century BC,'s court was adored with the philosophers of Kosala and Kuru-Panchala such as Ashvala, Jaratkarava-Arthabhoga, Bujjya Lahyayanani, Vshasta Chakrayana Kahoda,Kausi-takeya, Gargi Vachakuari, Uddalaka Aruni and Videgha Sakalaya-Yajyavalkya Vajaseneya, who was a pupil of Uddalaka Aruni. In the Mahabharata the Mithila King is said to have sided with the Duryodhana because he had learnt the science of fighting with mace from the latter. Bhima and Karna are said to have conquered Mithila. One Karala Janak made a lascivious attempt on a Brahmin maiden leading to the overthrow of the monarchy and that was followed by the rise of a republic, the Vajjian confederacy. The Mahabharata and Ramayana mentions a great battle between Pratardana, King of Kasi and Janaka King of Mithila. The Vajjian confede-racy, were the off springs of a queen of Kasi.

The soil of Mithila is very fertile. It is very suitable for horticulture, especially for the cultivation of mango, lichi, banana, sugar cane and many fruits and flowers. That is why, present Muzaffarpur Distt. was originally called as 'Modfalampur', house of sweet fruits. Still Langra Mango, Shahi lichi and small Chinima Banana is grown and like by the people on the banks of Gandak river. Soil is good and suitable for lichi such types of lichi is nowhere grown except in Dehradoon. Through proper management of water, fish, makhana and singhara can be produced abundantly. Until recently fish from this area was exported to several parts of the country, but now the fish market of Mithila is inundated with fish from Andhra Pradesh. Makhana a rare commodity in the whole world grows in Mithila. According to scientists makhana is tremendously rich in protein, but there is no proper arrangement for its production.

The supply of water due to rains differs in different parts of Mithila, the average annual rainfall varies from 1202 mm to 1443 mm. The depth at which underground water is found also differs in different areas due to the structural differences in the soil.

Mithila is bounded on the north by the terai of Nepal which is linguistically, geographically and culturally just like Mithila and on the east, south and west by the Rivers Kosi/Mahananda, Ganga and the Gandak respectively.

Raja Janak

If there is such thing as a spiritual and divine light, if there is righteousness in the heart there will be beauty in character. .. be when divine co-existence will be idyllic spiritual way of life throughout the world.

In the Brihad Vishnu Puran Mithila has been described in the Mithila Mahatmya in the Second Chapter, The Shloka 20-21 about is as under:

"Mithila Tairbhuhischa Vaidehi Naimikananm

Jnankhestra Kripapitha Swarn Langal Paddhatiah.

Janaki Janmbhumischa Nitpeksha Vikalmasha

Ramanandkari Vishvabhavini Nityamangala."

Meaning thereby Mithila. Tirbhukti, Vaidehi, Naimikanan, Jnanshila, Kripapeetha, Swarn Langal Paddhati, Janaki Janmbhumi, Vikalmasha, Ramanandkari, Vishvabhavini and Nityamangala are 12 names of Mithila.

Mithila's meaning:

"Antarvahyascha Sarvatra madhyante Ripavah sada

Mithilanam Sajneya Janakasch kritamahi.

Makaro Vishwakarta cha Thakarsthitipalakah

Lakaro laykarta vai trimara Shaktyobhavan."

(Inside and outside, who churn out enemies always Mithila be understood that where Janaks were ruling the land.

'Mi's Makar signifies Founder of the world and 'Thi's Thakar signifies Who looks after 'La's Lakar signifies the Destroyer and Trimatra is for the Power."

After 71 Chatryugi one Indra comes to throne who reins 3,67,20,000 human years. He is called Manu and Manawavtar is the time frame. Such 14 Indras are coming to throne.

Those live very long are called CHIRANJIVI. At present there are 8 CHIRANJIVIS i.e. Ashwatthama, Bali, Vyasa, Hanuman, Bibhishan, Kripacharya, Parshuram and Markandeya.

During the 24th Chaturyugi Brahma asked Vashsitha to go to Mrityubhuvan for becoming priest of Suryavanshi Kings. Vashishtha protested that Purohiti is prohibited profession. Then Brahma said that Lord Vishnu Himself would take birth at that Suryavanshi kings in Tretayug. Vashistha then said that he would go but wanted one correction.

Brahma asked what correction?

Vashishtha said, "You say Ramavatar will be in Treta. Now Satyayug is going on, then Dwapar will come and then Treta will come. I cannot live for so long in Mrtyubhuvan as: Satyayuga is of 1,72,800 years. Dwapar is of 12,96,000 years. Treta is of 8,64,000 years, and Kaliyug is of 4,32,000 years. If you make treat after Satyayug, I may go."

Brahma accepted that and since then Treta is coming after Satyayuga. Before that 24 times Satyayuga was followed by Dwapar and then Treta. On the acceptance by Brahma, Vashishtha came to Mrityubhuvan and became priest of Suryavanshis.

Suryavansis

The son of Sun was Manu who had four sons- 1. Ang, 2. Bang, 3. Nimiya and 4. Awadh on whose names were named Angdesh, Bangdesh, Nepaldesh and Awadh.

After Satyayug, came Tretayug when Rama was born but how he could marry Sita of his own Gotra and Dynasty and hence, Brahma had to make a way.

One day Brahma distracted mind of Nimiya who requested Vashishtha to have a *Yajna* so that he could reach *Swarag* with the body as Kaliyug's time cycle had been only 5,087 years. Vashistha replied, "OK", and he went his home. Nimaya started arrangements for *Yajna*. Seers were invited. All except Vashishtha was present on due time. A messenger was sent for him. Vashishtha became angry and said he had committed Indra before him for the *Yajna* and hence he was going to Indra. Knowing that Nimaya was in deep grief and proclaimed for the cancellation of *Yajna*. But all seers said that in the absence of Vashishtha, the *Yajna* be held with appointing Gautam as Acharya. Gautam started *Yajna*. That time kings had the *Gotra* of Gurus and so now Nimiya's *Gotra* was changed to Gautama from Vshistha and *Yajna sankalpa* was for 500 years. When Vashishtha returned from Indra's place, his son Shaktiji informed him the matter. Vashishtha reached Nimiya's place and both had hot talks. Vashishtha taking water in his hands gave curse, "Sadyah Videho Bhava". Nimiya also cursed him. With the curse of Vashishtha, Nimiya died. With the curse of Nimiya Vashishtha reached Varun's place seeking life by "Parkaya Pravesh". Varun listening to his prayer gave place to Vashishtha's soul in his heart and since then was known as Mitravarun. Once, Mitravarun had sperm fall seeing the nymph Urvashi. That sperm was kept in a Ghat. Agastya was born to that and hence he is called Ghat-Yoni utpanna. Some sperm fell on the Lotus leaf from which Vashishtha was born who is called a Veshyaputra.

After the death of Nimiya, he was asked to remain as hair above the eyes (Eye-brows- the *Nimi*) seers churned out a son (*Mathi Kaya*) of his dead body who was hence, called *Mithi*. *Mithi* established a good capital, which was named on him as Mithilapuri. Being born of the body of father he took title of Janak. Since that day whoever be the king was called Janak. Father of Sita was 21st Janak. He was named Kushadhwaj. In that Nimi's *Yajna* 19 seers came from the different parts of the country who settled down in Mithila whose sons are called from that *Gotra*. Due to change of *Gotra* and body Rama's marriage could be held with Sita.

According to Panini, where enemies were eradicated out that country was called Mithila. The people there had been with valor. Siradhwaj Janak under whose time Jagdamba Janki took reincarnation had defeated the King of Sakanshya. There had been 57 kings in the dynasty of Videh Janak. People use to live long in those days.

By the time of Dwapar that kingdom was weakened and was divided in the East and West Mithila. Hence, Western Mithila (Tirhut) accepted the ascend of Hastinapur and had sided with Kauravas during Mahabharata but Eastern Mithila (Matsya Janapada's) King Virat had sided with the Pandavas. Viratnagar was his capital where Pandavas spent secretly their period of their *Agyatvas*.

The last King of Janak Dynasty was of bad character, hence, the public under the leadership of Acharyas dethroned him and Mithila remained Kingless for hundreds of years for want of a suitable person. In fact, Mithila was the first democracy of the world, which worked on the basis of a Panchayati system under the guidance of Acharyas. People were disciplined afraid of Dharmadand. It was said:

"Na Raja Na Cha Rajyasit, Na Dandyo Na Cha Dandika

Dharme naiv praja saevaih Rakshantim parasparam."

Meaning thereby there was neither king, nor punishment nor punishment giver- the subjects were disciplined by the fear of Dharmdanda and were safe.

Including Vaishali in whole of the Mithila such state continued for long. Then outsiders started attacking. It was not difficult to defeat the simpletons of Mithila and Vajjisangh, Lichhavis, Shaishunag, Nand Dynasty, Shung Dynasty, Kant Dynasty, Gupta Dynasty, Vardhan Dynasty etc. ruled there from time to time.

In the same time period (5th-6th century) Jaywardhan Raja Salhesh became who made his capital at Mahisautha-Sirha (presently in Nepal which as then limited to the Kathmandu valley and nearby hilly terrains).

Tibetans had attacked on Mithila several times which was successfully defended by King Salhesh. Hence, he was called Shailesh (king of Mountains) from Jaywardhan which in local dialect was called Salhesh. His valor could make whole north-eastern India safe.

Sitamarhi

According to a story in the Brihad Vishnupuran, the Place where Janki was found, was Sulakshanapuri and there is Urvaja Kund, which is presently at Sitamarhi.

"यज्ञस्थल नरेन्द्रस्य यत्र लांगन पद्धतौ।
समुत्पन्ना महाभाग सीता राघव वल्लभा।
जानकेन, गष्हे सीता साक्षात् माया स्वरूपिणी,
तद्विषेशफलं सर्व काम प्रदायकम्।
तस्मिन् यज्ञस्थले चैत्र माधवे च मुमुक्षभिः।
यत्रा कार्य विषेशण द्वर्यो जन्मदिनंयत्।।
पूजनं दर्षन चैव पुराण श्रवणादिकम्।
ये कुर्वन्तिनरास्तत्र पुनर्जन्म न विद्धते।।"

(*Yagyasthal Naredrasya Yatra Langal Padhtau*
Samutpanna Mahabhag Sita Raghav vallabha
Janken, grihe Sita Sakshat Maya Swaroopni
Tadwishfalam sarv kam pradayekam
Tasmin Yagya Isthale chetra Madhve cha mumukshbhi
Yatra karye visheshn dwaryo janmdinmyat
pujan darshan chaiv puran shravandikam
ye kurvantinarstra punarjanm vidwate)

Pantpkhar

It is 8 k.m. north east of Sitamarhi. It is said that after her marriage Sita was carried in a palanquin to Ayodhya by this route. An old banyan tree is still standing here witnessing that sita had rested under this tree for a while. Land around Panthpakhar is very fertile due to the fact that Sita had dropped some paddy which was given by her mother Sunaina at the time of her *Bidai* as an old custom given to every bride in Mithila region. The bride drop some of paddy believing that she will not carry everything from her parents house and pray that dropped paddy in the field may fill the house of her parents next year.

Haleshwarnath Temple

This temple of Lord Shiva is 3 k.m. north west of Sitamarhi. As the myth goes the king Janak had founded a temple of Lord Shiva on the occasion of *Putra Yesthi Yajna*. This temple was named as Haleshwarnath Temple. On every Shivratri a great fair is held here.

Punaura Dham

Punaura Dham is about 5 k.m. west of Sitamarhi. Saint Pundrik's Asram was situated here. This place is the adjacent place claiming the honour of being the birth place of Goddess Sita.

Mithila region of north Bihar is surrounded by many rivers. It has been said in the Brihad Vishnu Puran they are all childhood friends of Janki, the daughter of King Janak.

1. **Dugdhawati River:-** It is said that when the king Janak brought the small child Janki who was found during ploughing, the holy cow Kamdhenu had herself offered milk to the small child. When Sita was taking milk, the milk flowed from both sides of her mouth and fell on the ground which turned into the river which is now known as Dugdhawati River. People who offers prayers on its bank gets salvation and released from sin and damnation.

2. **Kaushiki River:-** Kaushiki was daughter of the king Gadhi and sister of the saint Vishwamitra. She was married to saint Richik and was blessed with three sons. One of her son Sunahshep was sacrificed by the king Ambrish in a Yagya. Mother Kaushiki could not bear this and died. The tears which flowed from her eyes turned into a river called kaushiki.

3. **Triyuga River:-** Menka was wife of Himalaya. Menka Sister was Triyuga. Who was one of the friend of Janki.

4. **Kamla River:-** Kamla was the daughter of the Mandranchal Mountain. She prayed the Himalayas and got the boon that when anybody takes bath will get the same fruits as that in the river Ganges. She was the childhood friend of Sita. When she was a maid servant of a Brahmin, requested him to offer some rice to the Ganges river on her behalf. In the course of time he forgot to offer rice in the Ganges. While returning home he forgot the right path, after sometime he realized his fault and returned to the Ganges river and offered rice. To his utter

surprise the Ganges took rice from him by her own hands. After returning home he asked his maid servant Kamla about her true identity and asked to forgive him as he has taken her services as maid servant. Kamla turned into a river after giving him her true identification. People still go for Parikarma every year and gets boon. It is said that whoever recites the following twelve names Kamla river in the morning gets the blessing of Lord Sita and Rama. They are as follows: Kamla, Mandri, Punya, Haimi, Bhumisutaakhi, Kaliganga, Avdipatni, Kamda, Papharni, Gyanda, Muktido, Karmabandh vimochini.

5. **Narayani River:-** Narayani has three different names- Narayani, Gandki and Shaligrami. Daughter of Pushpdant was always praying on the Himalays and after getting boon was turned into river. In her childhood she used to play with Janki and started flowing in Mithila region. She is as pure as Brahma. Whoever takes bath in this river gets purified and directly go the heaven.

6. **Lakshmana (Lakhandei) River:-** This river is flowing at the birth place of Janki at Sitamarhi. She is the daughter of the sea and like Goddess Lakshmi. In the Brihad Vishnu Puran it is written as–

"*Tatha Sa, Lakshmana gaya maha patak nashini*

Samudratanya sakshat swannya Lakshmi Prakritata"

7. **Adhwara River:-** Daughter of saint Tirth who after much praying turned into Adhwara River and has played in childhood with Janki. People who drinks water of this river leaves all his bad habits and gets salvation after freeing from all his sin.

8. **Vanghosha River:-** She is daughter of saint Shandilya and prayed for thousand years and after getting boon turned into a river and became friend of Janki and played water game. This river fills the whole forest with the flowing sound of "Kal-Kal" hence is name is Vanghosha.

9. **Mandana River:-** This river also played with Janki in her childhood. She beautified the forest hence her name Mandana. One who dies at the bank of this river is freed from rebirth. People who takes bath on the day of "Kumbha Sankranti" gets all the fruits as that of all the pilgrimages.

10. Yamini River:- In ancient times Yamini was the daughter of Tapandari. Who prayed for the thousand years and fasted and inhaled only air. The whole world started burning from his prayer and there was lot of hue and cry therefore she was also called Ghoswati. She was the Sister of God 'Yam'. She used to give rest to Janki and was one of her friends. People get special fruit when they take bath in the month of Kartik. The river is so pure that once a crow dropped a piece of meat left by tiger who killed a cruel thief Durashaya, between the river yamin and Dugdawati was taken by God in Puspak Viman to the Haven.

11. Dhumra River:- Dhumra was the daughter of a milk man named Sukal living in Tapovan. When she was praying deeply a collection of smoke arose and spread in all direction. All the Gods were pleased gave a boon to flow like Dhumra River and play with Janki.

12. Virja River:- Virja was the famous daughter of a milkman named Vir. One who takes dip in this river in the month of 'sravan' goes directly to the heaven. She is one of the prominent members of the friend club of Janki.

13. Bagmati River:- Bagmati river originates from Kathmandu (Nepal). One who drinks water of this river gets freed from all his sin. This river was always in the service of Janki.

Sankirtan

Sankirtan Mahayajna: A few framed photos of Sita, Rama, Hanuman: Shiv Sanker, Vishnu, Brahma etc. are kept in a small Mandap which is erected for the purpose of *Sankirtan*. At this place, a batch of five persons come and recite the words "Sita Ram" with *Dhol* (drum) and *Jhal* while singing "Sita Ram" like the first and in this way twelve batches appear one after another within twenty four hours. In this way the *Sankirtan* continues throughout the day and night without any break. The singers of the *Sankirtan* belong to various castes viz. Bania, Teli, Brahman, Rajput ere. Here it is noteworthy that in these batches there is not a single local *Sadhu*. In each batch there is a leader or the in-charge of the party. The members of the batch get Rs. one per hour. He may be paid Rs. two or one kilo of rice as he likes for two hours. Besides these paid persons, some people voluntarily join this *Sankirtan*.

Sacred Parikarma (Circumambulation)

It is the circumambulation of sacred sites. In Nepal, Janakpur is the only place where Hindu pilgrims go for *Parikrama* which is attached great religious significance. According to the Mithila Mahatma (Ch. III) of the Brihad Vishnu Purana, describes (verses 29) three types of *Parikrama*, which are followed by the Janakpur pilgrims even today. These three types of Parikarmas are:

a) Bhrihad or (big) *Parikrma*,

b) Madhyam (middle) *Parikrama*, and

c) Laghu (small) *Parikrama*.

The circumference of Brihad *Parikrama* is 84 *Kos* or about 272 kilometers, in which whole of the Mithila region is circumambulated.

According to the Mithila Mahatmya (Ch. III. Verses 37), those who are unable to perform big circumambulation, should undertake this middle circumambulation. Presently, within this *Parikrama*, pilgrims have to move 40 *Kos* or about 128 kilcmeteres within this 15 sacred shrines are visited and takes fifteen days.

Laghu *Parikrama*, also known as Antargriha *Parikrama*, which is about 8 kilometers and takes 4 to 5 hours to complete one circle.

Ashtavakra

Ashtavakra was a famous scholar of the early Vedic period. He is known for his composition of The Ashtavakra Gita which is considered to be a standard work on Advaita Vedanta or theory of monism. The Ashtavakra Gita or the Song of Ashtavakra, also known as Ashtavakra Samhita is a scripture which documents a dialogue between the teacher, Ashtavakra and the student, Janaka, the King of Mithila. This work was often quoted by Sri Ramakrishna, his disciple Swami Vivekananda and Bhagavan Ramana Maharshi. It was held in very high esteem by Dr Radhakrishnan and by modern thinkers like Osho and Sri Sri Ravi Shankar. According to tradition, he was born to Kahoda and Sujata both of whom were students of Uddalaka and also related to him. Sujata was Uddalaka's daugher, while Kahoda was originally his student, whom he made his son-in-law, impressed by his excellent qualities. Nothing much is known about the life of Ashtavakra except that he was born in a family of eminent teachers and that he himself was the teacher of Patanjali, the author of Yogasutras. According to tradition he was a precocious child who was born with eight deformities, which earned him the name Ashtavakra. It is possible that he received his initiation into Advaita Vedanta from his eminent grandfather Uddalaka, who was one of the early authoritative sources on the subject. Uddalaka Aruni belonged to a special group of priests known as Charakas. The Charakas were wandering teachers who traveled from one part of the country to another spreading the knowledge of the Vedas and very popular for their knowledge and teaching ability. The young Ashtavakra must have spent considerable time traveling with his parents and grandparents and learning the secrets of the Vedanta from them.

The story of Ashtavakra occurs in the Vana Parva of Mahabharata. Ashtavakra means one who is deformed in eight places. His body got deformed in eight places due to a curse uttered by his father when Ashtavakra was still in the womb of his mother. When in his mother's womb, Ashtavakra overheard his father Kahora reciting the Vedas. Though still an unborn he already knew the scriptures, and hearing his father's mistakes, he called out to correct him. Kahora felt insulted and cursed the yet to be born child. In due course the male child was born with deformed limbs. Some years later, at the court of Janaka, Kahora engaged in a debate with the great scholar Bandin, son of King Varuna. Kahora was defeated, and Bandin had him drowned.

When Ashtavakra was twelve he discovered what had happened. He went at once to Janaka's court where he won over Bandin in a debate. Bandin then explained that his father had not been drowned, but had been banished to the bottom of the sea to serve King Varuna. He released Kahora, who wished at once to lift the curse from his son. He told Ashtavakra to bathe in the river Samanga. When he came out of the water, his body was straight.

The Ashtavakra Gita was composed in the form of a dialogue between Ashtavakra and King Janaka on the nature of soul, the nature of reality, the cause of the bondage and the means of liberation. It contains 20 chapters and 298 verses of which some are spoken by Ashtavakra and some by Janaka in response to his teachings. It becomes clear from the composition that king Janaka became enlightened with just one hearing. The information contained in the text is very direct in its appeal and simple to understand.

Whatever may be the truth, the Ashtavakra Gita seems to be the work of a self-realized seer who has experienced oneness with the supreme self. Advaita Vedanta was subsequently made more popular by the effort and writings of Adi Shankaracharya.

Ashtavakra Gita, similar to the other two works of the Triad viz the Yoga Vasishtha and the Yoga Aphorisms of Patanjali presents the traditional teachings of Advaita Vedanta by making the human mind as the focal point of attention and reform, for self-realization. Thoughts of Ashtavakra are more faithful to the major Upanishads and their non-dualistic idealism.

Ashtavakra states that there is no such thing as existence or non-existence, right or wrong, or moral or immoral. He completely rejects the world of objects, emotions and thoughts perceived through the delusory body, mind and intellect and consequently reject the principle of Maya also. To him, there is no individual ego (*jiva*) nor a creator (*Isvara*) nor a universe (*jagat*) nor any delusion (*maya*) other than the one infinite Consciousness.

In the eyes of Ashtavakra, one's true identity can be discovered simply by recognizing oneself as Pure Existence and that as individuals we are the Awareness of all things. To Ashtavakra there is only one goal to be aimed at and reached which is Self Knowledge.

Instruction on Self-Realization

The text starts with three questions put by the student Janaka to the teacher, Ashtavakra:

1. How can knowledge be acquired?
2. How can liberation be attained?
3. How is renunciation achieved?

Knowledge means the realization of the identity of the individual self and the Supreme Self or Brahman which is Existence, Knowledge and Bliss absolute *(Sat-Chit-Ananda)*. Liberation means freedom from ignorance, all bondage and limitations which leads to the complete destruction of all misery and the attainment of supreme bliss. Renunciation means un-attachment to the pleasure and pain derived from worldly objects and even the joy of heaven, which is also impermanent.

It may be noted that renunciation is defined as un-attachment and it has nothing to do with giving up possessions, as usually understood. Even with no possession one need not be a renunciate, for he can identify himself mentally with possessions to have them or to reject them.

Un-attachment is neither indifference nor suppression of natural feelings of pleasure and pain. Attachment springs from a sense of duality, the individual on the one side and the world on the other side. The individual who consists of body, mind, and senses has also got Consciousness which enlivens all the other components of the body-mind-senses complex. The individual is Consciousness, identified with his own body-mind-senses complex, and regards all the other individuals and objects in the world as separate and different from him.

As long as this identification persists, the individual's relationship with the world outside will be based on duality or the sense of difference between the two. The individual is attracted towards the persons and objects he likes and is repelled by those whom he does not like. He derives pleasure out of those whom he likes and pain out of those he does not like. Thus pleasure and pain are rooted in attraction and repulsion, which in turn is based on duality. Once this concept of duality is dissolved into the concept of unity of Consciousness, our perspective of life will undergo a change. We will be viewing ourselves in others and others in ourselves and conclude that there is but one Absolute Existence.

Thus whatever is so far observed by the mind, it is all but a temporary superimposition on the Self. The Self in all is thus the only reality; the world as it appears is unreal and its reality is in the Self and not in its outer form.

Living in the world we are not aware of this truth about the reality and erroneously take the superimposed form as the only reality. This state of mind is called 'ignorance' and all our relationships in the world are thus rooted in ignorance and not on reality.

The concept of unity of Consciousness will revolutionize the relationship between the individual and the world and such Knowledge will make us realize that it is the Self, the one real existence in all that is the source of attraction to them. Hence Brihadaranyaka Upanishad says "It is not for the sake of the husband that the husband is loved, but for the sake of the Self that the husband is loved."

Ashtavakra replied to Janaka "If you aspire after liberation, my child, reject the objects of the senses as poison and seek forgiveness, sincerity, kindness, contentment and truth as nectar."

Attachment to worldly objects is a great bar to spiritual progress and hence they should be shunned as poison at the outset which also implies the necessity of a total control over sense-organs and mind.

Knowledge of the Self

This section is significant in the entire Ashtavakra Gita as it delineates in unequivocal terms The One Ultimate Reality, the Self as the 'One Self in all existence and all existence in One Self.' All that falls under the cause and effect system of the mind is nothing but the Self, misapprehended as the illusory world of names and forms. Here, the nature of Brahman is brought out for a direct and immediate apprehension of all the seekers. It says that distaste for sense-objects is liberation and passion for sense-objects is bondage; such is the nature of true knowledge. Mind alone is the cause of bondage and liberation. Peaceful mind leads one to liberation.

Passions and aversions are the qualities of the mind. The mind is never yours. You are pure intelligence itself, free from all fluctuations, and changeless. In you the universe manifests itself like the waves in the ocean. Be you free from the turbulence of the mind. The body composed of the constituents of nature comes and goes away. The Self neither comes nor goes.

This universe is nothing different from you. Therefore how can the ideas of acceptance and rejection arise in you? From where will there be birth, activity and the ego-sense in you? Totally give up the attitude of 'I am this" and 'I am not that.' Consider all is the Self and be desire less and happy.

It is through your ignorance alone that the universe appears to exist. In reality you are the One, other than you there is no individual self (*Jiva*) or Supreme Self (*Atman*). This section is concluded by a revolutionary advice that to give up meditation through meditation is the highest meditation. The meditator has become the meditated! Man has stepped into the Throne of God!

Special Instructions for Self Abidance

The unique State of Liberation is to end all our perceptions of the world and destroy all our desires for sense-objects in the Knowledge of the Self. Although many try in this venture only a few succeed in Self-abidance. Ashtavakra gives here the explanation for such failures and provides us with effective tips to correct our ways to avoid pit-falls on the path to our Spiritual Goal Divine.

1. His guidance is solely based on his theory that he does not recognize the existence of anything as God or the universe or the ego other than the One Transcendental Self. In this Absolute state there are no objects or thoughts and all our perceptions are mere imaginations of a confused mind. Therefore he says:

   You may read any number of scriptures, you may become extraordinarily proficient in their contents, may give any number of eloquent lectures on them yet you have only understood their word meanings and not the Truth that is indicated by them until you realize the State of Peaceful Self where there is no plurality *(swasthyam)*.

2. Although with no success. This continuous yearning of human mind implies our basic urge to realize our real nature which is nothing but Bliss. This is the explanation why no man is satisfied with what one already possesses. Man is never satisfied until he discovers his Real Nature beyond all objects of pleasure

i.e. beyond all activities, passions and desires and beyond all pluralities.

3. One who covets sensual objects is called sensual while the one who does not covet is called 'not-sensual'. But the one who does not accept or reject sensual objects is neither sensual nor 'not-sensual'. He is the wise man free from the pairs of opposites, like a child, and indeed is well established in the Self. The one who is attached to the world wants to renounce the world to avoid miseries. But the one who does not have any attachment is free from all sorrows and miseries even while living in the world.

4. Until and unless one's ego is completely obliterated even Brahma, Vishnu and Mahesvara happen to be the teachers they cannot help him to abide in the Self.

Basic questions such as "What is good or evil? Life or death? Freedom or bondage? Illusion or the world? Creation or dissolution? The Self or the not-Self? What is the rising or the vanishing of thought? What is the visible world, or the invisible? What is the little soul, or God Himself?" have been raised in the Ashtavakra Gita.

The answers provided are that we are all one Self. The Self is pure awareness. This Self, this flawless awareness is God. There is only God. Everything else is an illusion: the little self, the world, the universe. All these things arise with the thought 'I', that is, with the idea of separate identity. The little 'I' invents the material world, which in our ignorance we strive hard to sustain. Forgetting our original oneness, bound tightly in our imaginary separateness, we spend our lives mastered by a specious sense of purpose and value. Endlessly constrained by our habit of individuation, the creature of preference and desire, we continually set one thing against another, until the mischief and misery of choice consume us.

But our true nature is pure and choice less awareness. We are already and always fulfilled.

It is easy, says Ashtavakra, 'You are the clear space of awareness *(cidakasa)*, pure and still, in whom there is no birth, no striving, no 'I'. Then how do we recover our original awareness? How do we dispel the illusion of separation?

Ashtavakra tells us how to end our Self-estrangement. "Be happy. Love yourself. Don't judge others. Forgive. Always be simple. Don't make distinctions. Give up the habit of choice. Let the mind dissolve. Give up preferring and desiring. Desire only your own awareness. Give up identifying with the body and the senses. Give up your attachment to meditation and service. Give up your attachment to detachment. Give up giving up! Reject nothing, accept nothing. Be still. But above all, be happy. In the end, you will find yourself just by knowing how things are."

It would be perverse to suppose that just because Ashtavakra, with his non-dualism, considers meditation merely a distracting habit, he means us to abandon our practice. Of course, from the perspective of unconditional freedom, where nothing makes any difference, meditation seems a comically self-important waste of time.

But Ashtavakra makes it clear. The moment a fool gives up his spiritual practices, he falls prey to fancies and desires. God help the seeker who presumes that since he is already and always fulfilled, he can give up trying. It is all a matter of knowing.

We are all indeed already perfect, but until we know it, we had better deal with our ignorance, and that can't be done just by listening to words. It requires *sadhana*, trying, doing what we do not wish to do. It means long, hard self-effacing work. The heart of Ashtavakra's advice is not to give up our practice, but to abandon our strenuous lethargy.

Dealing with our ignorance also means, for almost all of us, finding someone like Ashtavakra to help us. We cannot easily break the spell ourselves. Here again, Ashtavakra is very practical. At least half of the book describes the nature of the master, the man who has found his way.

It is an austere and enchanting portrait. The master is a child, a fool, a man asleep, a leaf tumbling in the wind. Inside, he is utterly free. He does exactly as he pleases. Rules mean nothing to him. He doesn't care who makes fun of him, because he is always playing and having a wonderful time. He lives as if he had no body. He seems to walk on air. He is un-smudged, like the clear sky or the smooth and shining surface of a vast lake.

Summary of Teachings

There are two ways to live in this world. Either to watch and be happy or get involved the deeper the involvement, the greater the stress and the pain. Many religions teach us not to get involved, but just be a pure witness to what goes on inside and outside. The Buddhist practice of mindfulness is a step in this direction.

Not to get involved with *samsara* or remain passive is difficult for ordinary human beings, because we have the tendency to feel important, to be part of something, to identify ourselves with some event or movement or other people. The ego is so deceptive in its mechanism that it will somehow drag us into the middle of the worldly activities through some dubious means. We see this happening in many areas of our lives especially in the religious world.

If you see some religious people fighting for a religious cause or fighting for God physically or emotionally as if God is a helpless being or a political leader, who needs these people to protect his teachings, you can be sure of the play of the ego there. The snobbery of a religious man is a direct display of ego. The attempt of a few followers of a *guru* or spiritual person to prevent others from reaching him without the latter's instructions is an example of a puffed up ego. Possessive as ordinarily we are, these people want to own their religion or God or their spiritual masters!

Ashtavakra advises us not to get involved, but simply watch. This non-involvement should be practiced not in the physical sense but from a spiritual point of view. You can still get involved, settle disputes, help somebody, resolve someone else's problem, teach the religious scriptures or write about them or be an arbitrator or even fight for a righteous cause, but all this has to be done unemotionally, without any particular aim or desire, with detachment, without feeling important and egoistic or as a sacrificial offering to God. We know that without adequate preparation, without inner spiritual advancement and without proper training under an adept or enlightened person this is not simply possible.

- Know that you are neither the body nor the mind nor the senses, but pure witnessing consciousness.
- The world appears because of your ignorance and it will disappear when you truly know who you are.
- The whole reality is one. The duality between the subject and the object, the knower and the known arises because of ignorance.
- When you achieve the supreme state of non-duality by realizing that you are in everything and everything is in you and know who you truly are there is nothing that can bind you to this world.
- Abandon desire and gain and look on everything like a dream with dispassion, equanimity and detachment.
- Live with a sense of abandon, with an empty mind, freed from deliberate action, setting aside all preferences and pairs of opposites, without interest in action or inaction, renunciation or acquisition, gain or loss and the very need to become liber person who is at peace wherever he is.
- Know that you are God himself and that everything.

Kunala

It is said that Prince Kunala established a kingdom in the Mithila region on the Indo-Nepal Border. It might be the same place where the present village, Kunauli (earlier known as Kunal Gram) at the bank of Kosi river at Indo-Nepal Border is situated. There are some historical and archaeological evidences to support this claim.

Kunala or Kunâl (3rd Century B.C.) was the son of Emperor Ashoka and Queen Padmavati, and presumptive heir to Ashoka after Mahendra became Buddhist monk, thus the heir to the Mauryan Empire which once ruled almost all of the Indian subcontinent. While he was supposed to be the future heir to the empire, he was blinded by another of Ashoka's wives, Tishyaraksha, at a young age in jealousy. While he was not able to take the throne, his son, Samprati, became his heir.

Significance of Name

The name Kunal in Hindi, Arabic, Italian, and Spanish means "Eagle" or "Protector of the Skies", thus it meaning 'Kunal' symbolises the Eagle. The eagle means is the Black Eagle. Black Eagle , and Kunal is the name of a Himalayan bird, the 'Painted Snipes'. The meaning of Kunal in Sanskrit is "Lotus". Kunal also means "bird with beautiful eyes", "someone who sees beauty in everything" or "one with beautiful eyes".

Ashoka sent his son to Ujjain, there to be brought up and carry out his princely education, to become the heir to the throne of the Mauryan Empire.

When the prince was eight years old, the king wrote (in Prakrit) to the tutors that Kunala should begin his studies. One of Ashoka's wives who wanted to secure the succession to her own son, being then present took up the letter to read it. She secretly put a dot over the letter 'a', changed Adheeyu into Andheeyu—another word, meaning he must be blinded. Without rereading the letter, the king sealed and dispatched it. The clerk in Ujjayini was so shocked by the contents of this letter that he was unable to read it aloud to the prince. Kunala, therefore, seized the letter and read the cruel sentence of his father. Considering that as yet no Maurya prince had disobeyed the chief of the house, and unwilling to set a bad example, he stoutly put out his eyesight with a hot iron.

Alternatively, some stories explain that Kunala had been sent to Taxila to put down a rebellion, which he managed to do peacefully. But he was similarly blinded through the treacherousness of Ashoka's wife Tishyaraksha.

Years later Kunala came to Ashoka's court dressed as a minstrel accompanied by his favourite wife Kanchanmala. When he greatly pleased the king by his music, the king wanted to reward him. At this, the minstrel revealed himself as prince Kunala and demanded his inheritance. Ashoka sadly objected that being blind, Kunala never could ascend the throne. Thereupon the latter said that he claimed the kingdom not for himself but for his son. "When," cried the king, "has a son been born to you?" "Samprati" (meaning "Just now") was the answer. Samprati accordingly was the name given to Kunala's son, and though a baby in arms, he was anointed Ashoka's successor. However, when Ashoka died, Sampriti was as yet too young to rule. Therefore, Ashoka was succeeded by another, older grandson, Dasaratha. After the demise of Dasaratha, Samprati did indeed become Emperor.

A semi-fictionalized portrayal of Kunal's life was produced as a motion picture under the title Veer Kunal (1925). Ashok Kumar, a Tamil film was produced in 1941 based on the life of Kunala.

Another reference of Kunala comes from place called Kunal Pathri Temple (located in the Dhauladhar Ranges in Kangra District, Himachal Pradesh) which is rock pilgrimage near dharamsala. It is said that there used to live a great devotee of lord Vishnu named Kunala. This temple is dedicated to goddess Kapaleshwari. It has beautiful carvings of gods and goddesses. It is believed that the skull of Devi Sati (Dakshayani), the wife of Lord Shiva, fell here after being cut off by the Chakra of Lord Vishnu into fifty-one pieces, to stop the ferocious dance, Tandava Nritya, of Shiva carrying the corpse of *Sati* (Dakshayani).

Maithili Language

Maithili is spoken in the Mithila region of Nepal and India. It is the second most spoken language of Nepal (around 12%). Linguists have classified Maithili as one of the Indo-Aryan languages. It is an offshoot of the Indo-Aryan languages, which is a branch of the Indo-European languages. Early Indo-Aryan languages (2500 BC to 500 BC) developed from Vedic Sanskrit to Laukik Sanskrit. Middle Indo-Aryan Languages (500 BC to 1000 AD) developed from Pali (early Prakrit, 500 BC to 100 BC) to Prakrit (middle Prakrit, 100 BC to 500 AD), Apbhramsha (neo Prakrit, 500 AD to 900 AD) and Avhattha (neo regional Prakrit, 900 AD to 1100 AD). From neo-Magadhi Prakrit and its variant Maithil Avahattha came Maithili language (1000 AD). It is in the category of Modern Indo-Aryan Language (1000 AD to till date). Linguists consider Maithili to be an Eastern Indic language.

According to the 2001 census in India, 12,179,122 people speak Maithili. Maithili has 35 million (2000) native speakers in the world. In 2003, Maithili was included in the Eighth Schedule of the Indian Constitution, which allows the language to be used in education, government, and other official contexts. Maithili has a rich literary and cultural heritage.

The first grammar of Maithili was written in 1880–81. A. F. Rudolf Hoernle published a grammar of the eastern Hindi from London in 1880 and compared with the other Gaudian languages. In this grammar, Dr. Hoernle recognized Maithili as a dialect distinct from Hindi. He was able to give some specimens of its grammatical forms, but no published materials were then available. The mis-classification by early linguists led to language politics in respect of Maithili. Beames (1872/reprint 1966: 84-85) considered Maithili as a dialect of Bengali. Grierson, however, adopted the notional term "Bihari" for the language used in Bihar; it has since been shown to be a misnomer for Maithili.

Maithili is derived from Avahattha, the Maithili Apabhramsha, which is derived from Magadhi Apbhramsha.

Maithili was traditionally written in the Maithili script (also known by the names Tirhuta, i.e., Mithilakshar) and Kaithi script. The ISO of Unicode Technical Committee has approved the encoding of Kaithi and Tirhuta scripts. Nowadays, Devanagari script is most commonly used. An effort is underway to preserve the Maithili script and to develop it for use in digital media by encoding the script in the Unicode standard, for which proposals have been submitted by Sh. Anshuman Pandey (now it has been approved by the ISO, the Unicode Technical Committee).

The term Maithili comes from Mithila, which was an independent state in ancient times. Mithila is important in Hindu mythology, since it is regarded as the birth-place of Goddess Sita, the daughter of King Janaka of Mithila, who eventually gets married to Lord Rama.

The most famous literary figure in Maithili is the poet Vidyapati (1350–1450), who wrote his poems in the language of the people, i.e., Maithili, at a time when state's official language used to be Sanskrit and Sanskrit was still being used as a literary language. The use of Maithili, instead of Sanskrit, in literature became more common after Vidyapati.

Literature

The main characteristics of Magadhi Prakrit is to mutate 'r' into 's', the 'n' for n, of 'j' for 'y', of 'b' for 'y' In the edicts of Ashoka the change of 'r' to 'h' is established. Mahavira and Buddha delivered their sermons in the eastern languages. The secular use of language came mainly from the east as will be evident from the Prakritpainglam, a comprehensive work on Prakrit and Apabhramsa-Avahatta poetry. Jyotirishwar mentions Lorika. Vachaspati II in his Tattvachintamani and Vidyapati in his Danavakyavali have profusely used typical Maithili words of daily use. The Maithili script, Mithilakshara or Tirhuta as it is popularly known, is of a great antiquity. The Lalitavistara mentions the Vaidehi script. Early in the latter half of the seventh century A. D., we find a marked change in the north-eastern alphabet and the inscriptions of Adityasena exhibit this change for the first time and hence forward the eastern variety develops by itself and becomes the Maithili script–a script which ultimately comes into use in Assam, Bengal and Nepal. The earliest recorded epigraphic evidence of the script is to be found in the Mandar Hill Stone inscriptions of Adityasena (c. 7th century A. D.), now fixed in the Baidyanath temple, Deoghar.

The Kamarupa dialect was originally a variety of eastern Maithili and it was, no doubt, the spoken Aryan language throughout the kingdom which then included the whole of Assam valley and whole of North Bengal with the addition of the district of Purnea. The language of the Buddhist Dohas is described as belonging to the mixed Maithili–Kamrupi language.

Vidyapati' 'Thakur' (1352–1448 appox.), also known by the sobriquet *Maithil Kavi Kokil* (the poet cuckoo of Maithili) was a Maithili poet and a Sanskrit writer. He was born in the village of Bisfi in Madhubani district of Mithila Region of India and Nepal. He was son of Ganapati. The name Vidyapati is derived from two Sanskrit words, *Vidya* (knowledge) and *Pati* (master), connoting thereby, *a man of knowledge.*

Vidyapati's poetry was widely influential in centuries to come, in the Hindustani as well as Bengali and other Eastern literary traditions. Indeed, the language at the time of Vidyapati, the prakrit-derived late abahatta, had just began to transition into early versions of the Eastern languages, Maithili, Bengali, Oriya, etc. Thus, Vidyapati's influence on making these languages has been described as "analogous to that of Dante in Italy and Chaucer in England."

Vidyapati, Maithili Poet

Vidyapati is as much known for his love-lyrics as for his poetry dedicated to Lord Shiva. His language is closest to Maithili, the language spoken around Mithila (a region in the north Bihar and region surrounding Janakpur in Nepal), closely related to the abahattha form of early Bengali.

The love songs of Vidyapati, which describe the sensuous love story of Radha and Krishna, follow a long line of Vaishnav love poetry, popular in Eastern India, and include much celebrated poetry such as Jayadeva's Gita Govinda of the 12th century. This tradition which uses the language of physical love to describe spiritual love, was a reflection of a key turn in Hinduism, initiated by Ramanuja in the 11th century which advocated an individual self-realization through direct love. Similar to the reformation in Christianity, this movement empowered the common man to realize God directly, without the intervention of learned priests. Part of the transformation was also a shift to local languages as opposed to the formal Sanskrit of the religious texts. The songs he wrote as prayers to Lord Shiva are still sung in Mithila and form a rich tradition of sweet and lovely folk songs.

Folklore says that he was such a great devotee of Lord Shiva that the lord was really pleased with him. And once He decided to come to live in his house as a servant. As the servant He is said to have taken the name Ugna. At several places in the region, Lord Shiva is still worshipped by this name. It is said that the lord in form of servant had imposed a condition on Vidyapati that he could not disclose his identity to anyone else or else he would go away. When Vidyapati's wife was angry at her servant and started to beat him

Vidyapati could not tolerate the same and asked his wife not to beat Lord Shiva himself and since then the lord disappeared and never was he seen again. According to the local legend, Vidyapati was an ardent devotee of Shiva. He composed several songs in the form of Nacharis and Maheshbanis to please the Lord. Impressed with the devotion and poetic creativity of the poet, Lord Shiva came to him in a disguised form of a cowherd boy called Ugna.

Ugna requested the poet that as he was an orphan boy he wanted to work in his house as his servant. With a little hesitation, the poet assigned him the job of looking after his cattle. Ugna became a very charming and affectionate servant to the poet within a very short period. One day, Vidyapati received an invitation to participate in a royal function of the king of Mithila, Shivasimha. He took Ugna with him and they left for the king's capital. On the way the poet became very thirsty but it was a huge barren land where he saw no drops of water.

The helpless poet finally requested Ugna to bring some water. Ugna too showed his inability to bring the water and requested him to travel some more distance, but Vidyapati refused to walk further and became unconscious. He fell on the ground. Now, Ugna, who was none but Lord Shiva himself, took out a jug of water from his matted hair (*jata*), revived him to consciousness and gave the poet water to drink. The poet felt the taste of Ganga-water and immediately asked Ugna wherefrom he had brought it.

Ugna tried to make some false story but failed to do so. He wanted to keep it a secret and that's why he avoided deliberately the poet's query, but as Ugna wanted to avoid it, the poet's curiosity increased. Finally, he appeared as Shiva, in his original form, before the poet. Vidyapati touched his feet and took the dust of Ugna's feet into his hands. Ugna now warned him not to disclose the secret before anybody including the poet's wife Sushila. Vidyapati assured Ugna to keep this secret with him. According to the local legend, Vidyapati was an ardent devotee of Shiva. He composed several songs in the form of Nacharis and Maheshbanis to please the Lord.

Ugna remained with Vidyapati for many years and helped him miraculously in many critical situations. For instance, when

Shivasimha was arrested by Emperor Allaudin Khilji of Delhi, Vidyapati accompanied by Ugna, came to Delhi to get him released. Knowing that Vidyapati was a poet, Allaudin arranged a scholarly debate between Vidyapati and his own court-poet.

Vidyapati was told to respond either in Persian or a mixed language alone. The poet with the heavenly blessings of Ugna defeated the Sultan's poet and responded in poetry he had composed in the prescribed languages. Not only that, with the blessings of Ugna he got rid of many obstacles created by the Sultan and his men at Delhi and finally succeeded in getting his king released from the prison of Sultan.

Now the story takes a very sad turn. Once, the wife of Vidyapati assigned some domestic responsibility to Ugna, which he failed to deliver according to her given instructions. She became angry with him and started beating him with a broom. This erratic behaviour of Sushila made Vidyapati frustrated that Shiva, of whom he was a great devotee, should be abused and humiliated. He could not control himself and shouted, "Stop! What the hell are you doing? Ugna is none else but Lord Shiva." It is said, that very moment Ugna disappeared from there.

Now Vidyapati realised his mistake. He left his house and wandered through many temples, rivers and jungles in search of Ugna. Finally, Vidyapati found Ugna in Nandanvana. Shiva told him that he would not go back to his house but would help him whenever required. The place where Ugna appeared before the poet as God is known as Ugnaasthan. A small lingam was enshrined by the local devotees. Recently a temple has been made for that lingam. This story is known to each and every person of this region. For them it is history. Even today they worship Lord Shiva while singing the devotional songs of Vidyapati to please him.

Vidyapati lived in the second half of fourteenth century. The exact years are not known, but the Tithi was Kartik Dhawal (bright half) Trayodashi. The ancestors belonged to the Gadha Bisaphi family of Maithil Brahmins of Kashyap Gotra. The ancestry is traced as Vishnu Thakur –› Haraditya –› Karmaditya –› Devaditya –› Dhireshwara–› Jayadatta –› Ganpati –› Vidyapati.

Devaditya had seven sons. The eldest Vireshwar was the Minister for peace and War under the Karnata King of Mithila Mithila, Maharaja Sakrasingha. He was the author of Dharmshastra treatise *Dasakarmapaddhati*. His son Chandeshwar Thakur was a great scholar of Politics, Astronomy and Dharmshastra.

Influence of Vidyapati in Bengal

The influence of Vidyapati in Bengal was so intense that for a period of time he was considered a poet of Bengali literature. His songs were mingled with those of Chandi Dasa who spread the Vaishnavism cult. Romesh Chandra Datta goes on to prove that there is no chance of their having met and Chandi Dasa came much later and had immense influence of Vidyapati especially in the *Krsnakirttana*.

The following quote from Grierson (Maithili Chrestomathy, p. 34)

> "And now a curious circumstance arose, unparalleled I believe in the history of literature. (His songs) were twisted and contorted, lengthened and curtailed, in the procrustean bed of the Bengali language and metre into a kind of bastard language neither Bengali nor Maithili. But this was not all. A host of imitators sprang up notably one Basant Roy of Jessore, who wrote, under the name of Vidyapati in this bastard language, songs which in their form bore a considerable resemblance to the matter of our poet, but which almost entirely wanted the polish and felicity of expression of the old master-singer. (These imitation songs known as "*Brajbuli*" songs) became gradually more popular amongst the Bengali people than the real songs of Vidyapati."

History of Brajbuli Literature by Dr. Sukumar Sen gives a complete account of "Brajbuli" poets. It is interesting to note that Ravindra Nath Tagore was so influenced by Vidyapati that he wrote (1884) a number of poems in the guise of *Bhanu-Singh* and named it *Bhanu-Singh-Thakurera Padavali.*

Influence of Vidyapati in Assam

It was Sankara Deva who introduced Brajbuli (Maithili) to Assam. Vidyapati was considered a Vaisnava singer. Shankar Deva found a great instrument in Brajbuli or Maithili in spreading Vaisnavism and introduced it in Assam. In the history of Assamese, Brajbuli occupies an important place; it was able to lay the foundations of Assemese Literature. The Department of Hislororical Antiquities, Government of Assam, Guwahati first published this literature.

Influence of Vidyapati in Orissa

Bengal acted as the source of spreading Maithili to Orissa in the first half of 16th century. The earliest known Brajbuli poem in Orissa by Ramanand Rai, the famous poet and dramatist, is dedicated to Pratap Rudra Deva (1504-1532). Dr. Sukumar Sen has given a vivid description of the meeting of Ramanand with Shri Chaitanya Dev (1511-12). The master asked Ramanand to explain to him the aim of Vaisnava religion and philosophy. Ramanand went on explaining without ant success. Then he asked the master if he could recite a few poems. The influence was magical and the master was greatly moved on hearing only a few lines. Other Orissa poets in the 16th century are Champati Rai, Maharaja Prataprudra Deva, Madhavi Dasi, Kanhu Dasa and Murari. In the next century the names of Rai Damodara Das, Chanda Kavi and Yadupati Dasa are worth mentioning. Oriya Brajbuli is still unexplored.

Influence of Vidyapati in Nepal

Due to close proximity Nepal could not escape the influence of Maithili. Though the people of tarai better known as Madhesias (Madhya Desi) speak Maithili, historically nothing of importance is found. However the Malla Kings of Nepal themselves wrote in imitation of Vidyapati and induced many poets and musicians to do the same. Recently the Madhesias have been accepted as the citizen of Nepal and this is a positive sign of Maithili getting its rightful place in the Kingdom of Nepal. The poets and writers are quite active in the tarai region.

Mithila Paintings

Mithila painting, also known as Madhubani painting, is in its originality an art form practiced by the women of all castes and communities of the region. The women of this country from time immemorial have been involving themselves in the various forms of creativity. The best one can find in their creativity is the relationship between nature, culture and human psyche. Also they use only those raw materials, which are available easily in abundance in the locality they are surrounded with. Through folk paintings and other forms of art they express their desire, dream, expectation and amuse themselves. It is a parallel literacy by which they communicate their aesthetic expression. Their art of creativity itself can be treated as a style of writing by which their emotions, expectations, freedom of thoughts, in the maryada, etc. Their background, gender, aspirations, hope, aesthetic sensibility, cultural knowledge, etc., find expression in all possible forms of their art. What one needs is to know the level of their enculturation and mode of learning before talking or writing about their art, putting women in the center. No region of this great country is untouched with the creativity of the women. We see the example of phulkari in Punjab, warli in Gujarat, chikan embroidery in Lucknow, weaving in the North-east, kantha in Bengal, miniature paintings in the state of Rajasthan, kethari, sujani and of course mithila paintings in the Mithila region of Bihar and Nepal.

The Mithila painting is one of the living creative activities of the women of this region. It is a famous folk painting on paper, cloth, ready made garments, movable objects etc., mainly by the village women of Mithila. Originally it is a folk art, practiced by the women of all castes and communities, including the Muslims, on walls and floors using the natural and vegetable colors. Later some people took interest in it and motivated the women to translate their art from walls and floors to the canvas and now the new form has given this a very distinct identity in the art world as well as in the market. This folk art has a history, a cultural background, women's monopoly and distinct regional identification.

Mithila Geographically

It is completely flat and free from rock or stone. Its soil is the alluvial slit deposited by the river Ganges, rich, smooth clay dotted with thousands of pools replenished by the monsoon, the only reservoirs until the next monsoon. If the monsoon is late or scanty, the harvest is in jeopardy. But if the rain god is kind, the whole plain bursts into green from October to February, dotted with man-made ponds where beasts and peasants bath beneath ancient Vatvrikshas. Madhubani is the heartland where the paintings are more profuse than elsewhere. "The region's rich vegetation so impressed ancient visitors that they called it Madhubani, 'Forest of Honey' (Vequaud, Yves 1977:9)", the name of the most acknowledged district for this painting. In this mythical region, Rama, the handsome prince of Ayodhya and incarnation of the Vishnu, married princess Sita, born of a furrow her father King Janaka had tilled. Mithila is that sacred land where the founders of Buddhism and Jainism; the scholars of all six orthodox branches of Sanskrit learning such as Yajnavalkya, Bridha Vachaspati, Ayachi Mishra, Shankar Mishra, Gautam, Kapil, Sachal Mishra, Kumaril Bhatt and Mandan Mishra were born. Vidyapati, a Vaisnav poet of 14th century was born in Mithila the people rightly remember him as the reincarnation of Jaideva (abhinavajaideva). Karnpure, a classical Sanskrit poet of Bengal, in his famous devotional epic, the Parijataharanamahakavya gives an interesting account confirming the scholarship of the people of Mithila. Krishna tells his beloved Satyabhama, while flying over this land on way to Dwarka from Amravati, "O lotus-eyed one behold! Yonder this is Mithila, the birthplace of Sita. Here in every house Saraswati dances with pride on the tip of the tongue of the learned (Mishra, Kailash Kumar 2000)". Mithila is a wonderful land where art and scholarship, laukika and Vedic traditions flourished together in complete harmony between the two. There was no binary opposition.

Background

Like the diversity of India, its folk art also presents a huge canvas and depicts the cultural mosaics of this country in a very colorful style. This art can rightly be termed as an ocean of the folk art, which, since earliest times, has been fed by the rivers of popular artistic creativity–rivers that have flowed into it from all cultural-geographical pockets of the Indian sub-continent. The well-known grammarian, Panini, drew a distinction between artists–the *rajashilpi*, or craftsman employed by the court–and the *gramashilpi*, or village craftsman. Originally *shilpi* would seem to have been a term generally applied to the technically trained craftsman; later, however, it came to denote the artisan. Thus the writing concerning the theory of art are referred to collectively as the *shilpashastras*. Being for the most part of a highly schematic character, these manuals of artistic instruction could not, of course, be expected to include a description of folk art or of amateur art practiced by women at home. By and large they form part of orthodox ecclesiastical literature with art as the handmaiden of the courts of Brahmanic orthodoxy (Coomaraswamy, A.K. 1964: 33-34). But that did not cause any disturbance for the women and the commoners of India to practice various forms of creativity through various mediums on the occasion of rituals, altars, and festivals and also during the leisure period. The fellow villagers and locals always appreciated their creativity and innovation. As a result, in Sanskrit, as well as in the folk tradition, an artist is treated as a person with a magnetic ability to create a world of imagination. Metaphorically, an artist is always compared with the Gods. "In Hinduism, Vishnu has a thousand names, many of which refer to works of art. In Islam, one of the hundred names of Allah is Musawwer, the artist. The Sanskrit word *kala* (art) means the divine attributes which direct human acts and thoughts. Man, God and art are inseparable. Art is not removed from everyday life, it reflects a world view (Saraswati Baidyanath 1999:10) No distinction is made between fine and decorative, free or servile arts. The eighteen or more professional arts (*silpa*) and the sixty-four vocational arts (*kala*) embrace all kinds of skilled activity. There is no difference between a painter and a sculptor. Both are known as *silpi*. The term *silpa* designates ceremonial act in the Asvalayana Srautasutra, and in this sense it is close to karu, which in the Vedic context stands for a maker or an artist, a singer of hymns, or a poet. In a reference in the Rigveda, Visvakarma, a god of creation, is mentioned as dhatu-karmara, while karmara alone refers to artisans and artificers (Rigveda X.72.2; Atharvaveda III 5-6; Manu IV 215). Visvakarma is supposed to create things out of dhatu, "raw material", an act known as sanghamana (Rigveda X 72.2). The process of cutting, shaping and painting has been often explained in the text by the task."

In Mithila a woman does painting on the wall, surface, movable objects, and canvas; makes images of gods, goddesses, animals and mythological characters from the lump of clay; prepares objects such as baskets, small containers, and play items from sikki grass; does embroidery on quilt–popularly known as kethari and sujani; sings varieties of ritual and work songs. These artistic activities are done by a lady as a routine work that makes her a complete creative personality: a singer, a sculptor, a painter, an embroidery design maker and what not! Without knowing these primary details one may not understand the aesthetic wonder of Mithila paintings. From generation to generation the women of Mithila have produced a vigorous distinctive painting. That this traditional art has survived the innumerable vicissitudes of history is due, first of all, to the social organization of Mithila, one based on the village community, in whose corporate life the women have clearly understood roles. Beyond their extended families, the women artists work for a rural society with whose requirements they are perfectly acquainted. It is within this framework that the women continue to reproduce age-old forms; indeed countless recapitulations have resulted in an attitude of mind in which they can produce the most abstract designs without conscious effort. The possibility of any radical assertion of individuality in the modern sense is extremely limited. This communal village life is strengthened and sustained by the universal prevalence of social gatherings, traditional storytelling, dancing and singing festivities and ceremonies, processions and rituals.

In Mithila, painting is normally done by women folk in three forms: painting on floor, painting on wall and painting on movable objects. Aripan, under the first category, is made on the floor with the paste of *arva* (crude) rice. This rice paste is called pithar in the local language. Apart from the floor it is also made on banana and *maina* leaves and *pidhi* (wooden seats). A woman or a girl does it using her right hand's fingertips. In tusari *puja*, a festival celebrated by the unmarried girls in order to please Gauri and Shiva to have a suitable husband; an aripan is made with dry rice powder in white, yellow and red colors. Aripan is of different types suiting different occasions. Astadala, sarvatobhadra, dasapata and swastika are its main varieties. Wall paintings are multicolored. Three to four colors are usually used to depict the wall paintings. Pictures include those of nayana-jogini, purain, carrier of fish, curd, jack fruit, trees of fruits such as mango and pomegranate and birds like peacock. Attractive floral motifs adorn the wall on three sides of the entrance. Paintings on movable objects include those on clay models of pots, elephants, birds like Sama and chakeba; Raja Salhesa, bamboo structure, mat, fan and objects made of sikki. Decorative multicolored designs made on the faces of brides and the sumangalis also fall in this category. Many of these paintings have great *tantrik* significance. Certain non-Vedic rites during the marriage ceremony, practiced exclusively by the women, like thakka-bakka, nayana-jogini etc., are directly related to the Mithila tantra.

The tradition of wall paintings as well as surface paintings for beautification of dwellings and ritual purposes in Mithila is believed to have survived from the epic period. Tulsidasa in his magnum opus the Ramcharitamanasa gives a vivid account of Mithila painting decorated for the marriage of Sita and Rama. Influenced with the wonderful pair–Rama and Sita–Gauri, the Consort of Siva, desired to participate in the actual marriage ritual and wanted to paint the kohabar where the sumangalis had to perform songs and related rituals for this divine ideal couple. These decorations are mythological murals, added with deities of Hindu pantheon, besides regional flora and fauna. The women artists, according to the old age tradition, are the sole custodians who practice this folk painting passing down for generations from mother to her daughter. They have been retaining this great art form in the region since time immemorial. The girl learns to play with the brush and colors at an early age that finally culminates in the kohabar, which acquires great sanctity in the social life. All religious ceremonies relating to the marriage are performed in the kohabar. The ahibaatak patil is kept burning in all through for four days.

The present form of Mithila paintings, also called Madhubani paintings, are the translation of the wall paintings, floor paintings and terracotta idols on to paper or canvas. This experiment is not very old. In the late sixties, twentieth century, in order to create the job opportunity for the women to face the cruel challenge of the terrible drought, some women were approached to translate their art from walls, floors and other form of creativity to the paper or canvas. They did and it worked miraculously. At first when the ritual was fixed on paper it had a very small audience at the receiver's end but it certainly opened a new world of art appreciators and also potential buyers of their artworks in the world. This was a great success and a ticket to trade. Since then the painting medium has diversified. Wall paintings were transferred to hand-made paper (which was of poster size) and gradually it laid the way for other mediums and motifs like greeting cards, dress materials, sun-mica etc. The stylized figures, fierce lions with electrified manes, the human profiles reminiscent of ancient Cretan pottery, the bright native colors and all possible indigenous experiments appealed to the audience of the world. In the beginning only a few women were given the opportunity to practice this art but after ten years some women of the all casts also came forward with a new style. Till now, the women of the Harijans were not given the opportunity to experiment in this art with their hands. There is an interesting story behind this. The women of higher castes were not allowed in the region to cross the boundary of their houses, however they wanted to do some work for generating finance to run their family smoothly mainly during the natural calamities. One folk poet, Faturilal of present Shahpur village of Madhubani had described the pathetic condition of the people during famine in late nineteenth century in his famous poetry known as the Akalkavitta. Influenced with his poetic description the then Maharaja of Darbhanga, Maharaja Laxmeshwar Singh decided to create job opportunities with the help of the British ruler for the people. The women of lower castes however were helping their husbands or male counterparts by working in the agricultural fields of better off people and also as maid servant in the houses of higher castes. This time also some people thought of involving the women of higher castes in some creative business. Mahatma Gandhi's experiment with charkha came as a wonder for all the women. They found it very easy as earlier they were preparing cotton thread on tekuli for preparing the *janeu* or *jagyopaveeta*. The khadi workers used to give raw cotton to them in every house and collect their prepared yarns. Very delicate and costly khadi clothes are woven from these yarns today and they are in great demand everywhere in the country. Some women prepare such very fine thread that at times the length of a sacred thread is contained in the case of a piece of cardamom. Anyway, this created a space for women. Khadi centers used to give money as well as clothes for their labor This was a respectful job mainly for destitute, widows and poor women of higher castes in the locality. And the second experiment was Mithila paintings. As a result some women of such as Sita Devi contributed to promote the Brahmin style of Mithila paintings. This art, characterized by bright colors and an absence of shade, is mainly concerned with the khobars and gods and goddesses (Krishna, Rama and Durga mostly). Bawa Devi and her daughter, Sarita Devi later made important personal contributions.

Another social group, the women was also facing the similar problem. They were landless community and their women also got attracted towards this art form to gain some finance. They worked hard on the art and also in the entrepreneurship and finally achieved recognition in the seventies. These women earned their name for their elaborate line paintings. They cover their sheets of paper or cloth or any object with the care of cartographers, producing finished pictures where exquisite execution is more impressive in view of the difficult conditions in which they work. They depict village or religious scenes to the finest details such as the late Ganga Devi, Pushpa Kumari, Karpoori Devi, Mahasundari Devi and Godawari Dutta. These two forms of Mithila expression, both due to women from the higher castes, embody traditional Mithila art.

The third group, the Harijan women, came forward in the 1980s. The women of the Harijan community were doing all forms of traditional paintings and art forms for ritual purposes and also for decorating their dwellings. Influenced by the entrepreneurship and experiment they experimented the *godna* and other bright color in their depiction of paintings. Their pictorial alphabet began to include lines, waves, circles, sticks and snails, opening the way to stylization and more abstraction. That also worked. Jamuna Devi and Lalita Devi are famous Harijan female painters. Lalita Devi sews faces of deities like fruits; profusion of motives seems to rightly counter-balance the precariousness of existence, they transcend their daily lives to harvest new creations. And now women of all castes have been practicing this art as a job earning profession.

Being the folk of the villages, these artists rely on the kindness of nature for colors. It provides them with a wonderful range of natural hues derived from clay, bark, flowers and berries. The colors are usually deep red, green, blue, black, light yellow, pink and lemon. They create mood and hence played an important role. For instance, energy and passion find expression through the use of red and yellow, as monochrome crashed over large surfaces of the painting. Concentration of energy and the binding force is best reflected in red while green governs the natural leaves and vegetation. For the lower style of paintings, hand-made papers is washed in cow dung. Once the paints are ready, two kinds of brushes are used-one for the tiny details made out of bamboo twigs and the other for filling in or space is prepared from a small piece of cloth attached to a twig. In the beginning homemade natural colors were obtained from plant extracts like henna leaves, harshingar leaves, gamariya leaves, flower, bougainvillea, neem, etc. These natural juices were mixed with resin from banana leaves and ordinary gum in order to make the paint stick to the painting medium. Home-made paints, though cheap, was time consuming and produced less than the requirement. The solution was at hand to switch to the synthetic colors available aplenty in the market. Now colors come in powdered form, which are then mixed with goat's milk. Black was obtained from the soot deposits by the flame of *dibia* dissolved in gum.

The kohabar is replete with paintings based on mythological, folk themes, and tantric symbolism. The paintings in this chamber are designed to bless the couple. The central theme of all paintings is love and fertility, though the approach may vary. It can commence with the story of Sita's marriage or Krishna-Radha episode with the ecstatic circle in which he leads the *gopis*. The people of Mithila, also known as Maithils, are Sakti worshipers with the influence of tantric rituals and so Siva-Sakti, Kali, Durga, Ravana and Hanumana also appear in their murals. Symbols of fertility and prosperity like fish, parrot, elephant, turtle, sun, moon, bamboo tree, lotus, etc., are more prominent. The divine beings are positioned centrally in the frame while their consorts or mounts or simply their symbols and floral motifs form the background. The human figures are mostly abstract and linear in form; the animals are usually naturalistic and are invariably depicted in profile. It begins with the flow of the brush without any preliminary sketching. Though natural colors and twigs have given way to brushes and artificial paints, the subject of Mithila paintings has changed enormously.

The commercialization has caused serious harm to this art. The women and men are learning this art from the markets in towns and metropolitan cities. The trainers themselves do not know the essence and aesthetic beauty of this folk art and they teach their students in utter ignorance. Some of them do not know the color combination, obtaining the color from the nature, preparing the background, relationship between rhythm, color, songs, rituals, dance and the art of painting. The themes and designs of the paintings are, now, in most of the cases decided by the buyers. The buyer-centric approach has caused serious threat to the originality of color, design, motif, and sensitivity of this great art form. In the name of the tantric painting, we see the women have painted something very different from the tradition of Mithila. Commercialization of this art has created the interest of several males in it. They have been now also painting without knowing the significance of women in it. For them it is an industry that can easily provide a job opportunity for them. They are willing to paint anything as per the requirement of the buyers in the name of Mithila painting.

But when we talk about the Mithila painting as folk or traditional painting, which is painted on a ritual occasion or any ritual painting of India we see many activities are combined. This combination, in fact gives special significance to the art. "Viewed at the level of perception and experience, all these local, regional, macro pan–Indian, and beyond Indian expression of art emerge and are held together by an integral vision that makes life an art, part and parcel of a single totality where life functions and creative art are inseparably intertwined. Painting, music, dance, poetry, and other functional objects are inseparable from myths, rituals, festivals and ceremonies. There is no dichotomy between the sacred and profane, life and art. The human and the divine are in a continuum, in a constant movement of interpretation and transformation." When a painter paints a wall or a floor, she is supported by other women by way of singing songs and helping tunes. The lesson drawn from the folk stories and narratives also help her in painting the themes of various requirements. The tantric paintings for instance, are influenced by the famous narratives of the Madhusravani *katha*. This *katha* is narrated before a newly married bride on the occasion of Madhusravani for 13-15 continuous days by an elderly and experienced lady who is usually well versed in the art of narrative. She dramatizes the stories in a very lively manner and narrates the origin of earth and various tantric stories. This festival is celebrated with songs, dance, ritual paintings; spell of mantras, etc. One such complete folk-cum-tantric story of Manasa Debi is given below:

Manasa Debi is known as Bisahari and said to have extraordinary supernatural power to bless her devotees. She can also ruin and kill those who do not believe in her existence and offer their prayer to her. There was a very rich ship merchant, named Chanrakar. He was also known to the people as Chandu Saudagar. He was a great devotee of Siva. He had six sons and a happy family. He did not consider Manasa as a Goddess. Manasa Debi did not like this attitude of Chandu Saudagar and killed all his six sons by sending black snakes. However Chandu Saudagar did not relent. One day pleased with the devotion of Chandu Siva appeared in his dream and expressed his willingness to bless him with some great things as per the desire of Chandu Chandu Saudagar asked him for a son. Siva agreed to bless him with a son but put a condition before him. "If you want to have a son who will have long life, he would be a fool, lethargic and an idiot. Instead if you want to have an ideal, intelligent and handsome son he will die at the early age of 20", said Siva, "now you tell me what exactly you want." After a serious thought Chandu Saudagar opted for an intelligent son who would have a short life. Later, Chandu's wife gave birth to a male child whose name was Bala Lakshendra or Lakhinder. Lakhinder was bright, intelligent and a very cultured child. Everybody was happy with his behavior. When he reached the marriageable age his father wanted to solemnize his marriage ceremony with an equally qualified and highly cultured girl. After a great search, Chandu Saudagar saw Bihula. She was very beautiful, meritorious, highly cultured and a homely girl. Chandu also came to know that according to her family tradition every woman dies as a sumangali and none of them would become a widow at any point of time. In this family tradition of Bihula, Chandu Saudagar saw a ray of hope for his dear and affectionate son Lakhinder and as a result he immediately decided to choose her as his daughter-in-law.

The marriage was solemnized in a happy atmosphere. Lakhinder was bitten by a dangerous cobra at the behest of Manasa Debi on his first night of the bridal-bed in the bridal chamber itself. Lakhinder cried in helplessness and breathed his last. The innocent but firm Bihula decided to remain with his dead body on a raft in the river Ganges. Chandu and neighboring people made futile attempts to dissuade her. But she was determined. Finding no other alternative, Chandu gave permission to Bihula. She started her voyage on a raft along with her husband's dead body. The current slowly carried the raft. She had to face various difficulties in her journey, but she overcame them all. Ultimately she found a washerwoman washing the clothes by the side of the river Ganges. Her small child was disturbing her. Getting irritated with the behavior of her girl child, the washerwoman killed her baby and started washing her clothes. Once she had washed all her clothes, she sprinkled some drops of water on the face of her baby and the dead baby became alive. Bihula took no time to understand the supernatural power of this lady and took shelter at her feet and narrated the sad story to her.

In accordance with the advice of washerwoman, Bihula reached the Mahadeoloka with her. On the instruction of the washerwoman, Bihula performed a wonderful dance to please the Lord. The Lord was very impressed by her graceful performance and was moved by the story of her tragic life on earth and heaven. He called Manasa and asked her to give the reasons of her tragedy. Manasa vehemently denied that she was responsible for the tragedy of Bihula. However, Bihula succeeded in producing definite evidence. But Manasa insisted that she was not responsible for the sad plight of Bihula, and it was Chandu Saudagar, her father-in-law, who was solely responsible, because he always abused and disrespected Manasa Debi and did not consider her to be a goddess worthy of worship. Manasa then told Bihula that if Chandu Saudagar were to worship her, she would bring Lakhinder back to life. Bihula felt the hope of restoration of life for the corpse of her husband in the statement of Manasa and agreed to her proposal. Manasa then brought Lakhinder and other six sons of Chandu Saudagar back to life by chanting spells. At the humble request of Bihula, Manasa recovered all the boats of Chandu Saudagar along with the cargo and crew that had been submerged by the wrath of Mansa Debi. She thus fulfilled the desire of Bihula. With all the seven sons and lost property of Chandu Saudagar, Bihula came down to the city in the earth where the old eyes of Chandu Saudagar and his wife were counting the days to breathe their last. All of a sudden they received all their lost sons along with the cargo and crew.

Now Chandu Saudagar realized the power of Bihula and gave his consent to worship the deity–Manasa Debi. The goddess blessed him. He realized that there was none except Manasa Debi in these three worlds. Finally, he worshiped Manasa with offerings of various fruits and animals.

Thus, Chandu Saudagar, a devout follower of Siva, changed his religious ideas and became one of the staunch followers of the Manasa-cult, which was originally a tantric-cum-folk cult.

The other stories narrated during the Madhusravani are Satik Katha; Pativrata Sunaynak Katha; Bala-Basantak Katha; Gosaunik Katha; Chanai Bairsi Katha and Raja Srikarak Katha. The Madhusravani is celebrated in the rainy month of the *Savan*. Everywhere snakes and other poisonous insects are found in abundance. People try to please the deities and these serpent deities by way of offering puja, singing songs, celebrating festivals, invocating mantras etc., the place where the Madhusravani *katha* is narrated, is decorated with the ritual paintings. Some women sing some tantric songs during the decoration in a falsetto tone. Through the song the snake deity is being worshiped in order to bless the people, mainly the groom of the newly married bride.

The purpose behind folk narrative, narrated on the occasion of the Madhusravani is to explain the interconnectivity amongst various activities in the creation of a ritual art. This interconnectedness get lost when the art is experimented as a commodity and sold in the market in huge quantum. A lady when painting the wall does not expect any financial return from anywhere but when she paints in order to sell her painting as a commercial production, she becomes a sales girl. Her entire attention shifts from culture to consumerism and she puts herself in the mercy of her buyers. She paints not to retain tradition but to earn better livelihood.

In the last twenty years, in order to get job opportunities, a very huge population of Mithila has migrated to the cities and mega-cities of India and abroad. This is a continuous trend. Many of them have settled in those cities. They are emotionally attached with their ritual and tradition. Marriages are solemnized in these cities in the banquets and hotels. And no traditional marriage can take place without kohbara painting. These paper and cloth paintings therefore solve their purpose. Now they decorate the banquets, hotels or any other venues with the Mithila paintings and feel very much rooted in their tradition. Such development has given a new and potential group of buyers to the painters. Some individual painters i.e., Karpoori Devi, Ganga Devi and Jamuna Devi have innovated as per the requirements of their potential buyers. Ganga Devi has wonderfully depicted the Ramayana episode in her paintings.

Ganga Devi also depicted her journey from Madhubani, a small town in north Bihar to All India Medical Sciences, New Delhi she made in order to get treatment of cancer she was suffering from. The train, doctors, hospital, syringe, medical ward everything she drew delicately. Her innovations were excellent, appealing and unique in many respects. Some critics however did not appreciate such step thinking that it might disturb the originality of the folk painting of Mithila but majorities of them were in agreement with Ganga Devi. She did lose the originality of her style, brush, color, canvas and thought processes in her creativity.

Together with her brother Mitar Ram, but to a greater extent, Jamuna Devi has developed a brightly colored style that has no equivalent in Mithila art. Jamuna Devi is self-taught and no rules apply to her work that evokes children's play and raw art. She delights in portraying animals-cows, for example. Her representations of the sacred animals range from a parody of anteaters to a hybrid combination of dancing angels and juggling balls. Many of her paintings can be viewed upside down, showing her total freedom from conventions. But she is very strict to maintain the tradition in terms of obtaining color, preparing background of the canvas, depicting the pictorials etc. These painters paint landscapes, rivers, and any other things their customers want them to paint.

In the villages of Jitwarpur and Ratni the Mithila paintings have emerged as a commercial activity where children can be seen engaged in arranging the hand crafted paper or fetching the colors. These days Jamuna Devi teaches mithila paintings to more than 15 students free of cost.

Mithila painting is more than an art. Through this creative ability a group of women express their desires, dreams, expectations, hopes and aspirations to the people. For them their style is a kind of script through which they communicate with the male folk or with the people of the rest of the world. They are the creative writers who write their feelings through the medium of paintings. They are the creators and close to the god in the perfection. Because of money culture some men have also jumped into this creativity but in its essence and nature even today it is a women's creativity.

Makhana

Mithila is traversed by a number of perennial rivers and their numerous tributaries. It witnesses an average annual rainfall of 1200 mm. In this region the excavation of ponds through human efforts has been a socio-religious practice since time immemorial. Bowl-shaped physiography makes it a recurrent site of water-logging with no natural outlet. The natural water bodies in this area constitute the ox-bow lakes (*mauns*), thousands of depressions (called *chaurs*) etc. All these water bodies are utilized for rearing fishes and for cultivation of deep water paddy, *Makhana* and *Singhara*. Some other aquatic plants which grow wild and are consumed as subsidiary food items include–*Purain, Bhent, Saruk, Keasur, Chichorh, Khobhi, Karmi Saag, Kauathuthi* etc. Quite a good number of them also serve fodder to the cattle.

Of these, *Makhana* provides a means of sustainable development of the area, more particularly that of the fishing community belonging to the weaker section of the society and marginal farmers. Integrated aquaculture of fish with *Makhana* is the usual practice in this area. It has a significant bearing on the regional economy. It is cultivated as crop in Darbhanga, Madhubani, Saharsa, Supaul, Madhepura, Araria, Purnea and Katihar districts.

Cultivation of *Makhana* is localised in Mithila and to a lesser extent in lower Assam water bodies. Outside north Bihar and lower Assam it is available in wild form only. Association of wild Trapa fruits confirms its semi-wild status in Assam.

Approximately 4000 ponds in Darbhanga and Madhubani districts are utilized for growing *Makhana*.

Makhana (botanically known as Euryale ferox Salisb.) belonging to family Nymphaeaceae/Euryalaceae, is the major cash crop cultivated in the ponds with stagnant water. For the growth of *Makhana* plants a maximum of one meter deep water bodies are required in Kamala-Kosi and Ganga-Mahananda belt. These belts are more suited for growing this crop as compared to Bagmati and Gandak-Burhi Gandak belts.

The crop cycle starts with germination of seeds in December Passing through young stage the plants achieve the grand growth stage during May-June Around February-March the leaves face the attack of a blight which causes necrotic spots. Young plantlets are also attacked by *laahi* (i.e. the aphids). Farmers usually roll large ropes over the leaves. This leads to the death of insects by falling down in the water. During April the larvae of a leaf-roller insect also were found to form cases on leaf margins.

The plants mature by May-June. The leathery and spiny leaves overshadow the pond surface and, a good crop hardly leaves any open space on the surface of water. Fruits set around this period and start bursting upon maturity from June onwards till the crop is there in the pond. Arillated seeds float on the water surface for two to three days and then fall to the bottom. Flower of two types are produced by the plants (a) one is Cleistogamous, which does not open and also does not come to the surface. The other Chasmogamous ones open at the surface and go down after 2 to 3 days. Both the types of flowers are capable of seed-setting, which is very significant scientifically. Each plant produces 15-20 fruits each, with an average of 400-500 seeds. It is from the bottom that the seeds are taken out for popping. This is a very intricate process for which several dives have to be made.

Makhana farmers in Mithila do not allow the plants to stay in the ponds after August-September. This is because of the fact that the seeds have to be taken out from the bottom. For this, the spiny plants are to be uprooted first. It is not at all possible to do the harvest work with the plants still intact in the ponds due to dense spiny leaves. The plants, although reported to be perennial in various texts, behave as annuals in north Bihar ponds for all practical purposes. The perennial plants might be semi-wild botanically.

The seeds, left over at the pond bottom sprout during December-January to give rise to the next crop. A new pond has to be seeded either with fresh seeds or young plants are transplanted latest by March-April.

The *Makhana* ponds yield air-breathing, black cat-fishes like singhi, mangur, kawai etc. as additional produce. This is because these fish species engulf air by coming to the surface of pond water. The pond water suffers from depletion of dissolved oxygen, which makes it noxious for non-air breathing fishes.

The crop provides a definite impetus to the fishing community, who depend upon it for their livelihood. While the menfolk do the work related with pond, the women folk are associated with drying of seeds and their popping. The latter process is performed mostly during early morning hours, because the rise in day temperature is deleterious for pop-making.

The seeds yield pops, which are one third of the total seed weight. The pops have generally three grades and their prices vary accordingly. The raw seeds are also graded by the fishing community by using sieves withseven different mesh sizes.

The pops are transported outside north Bihar mostly through rail. The railways charge freight as per the space occupied. This leads to enhancement in the price of *Makhana*. The Grade one pop is beyond the reach of common man in this area because of its high price. At present it is selling at the rate of Rs. 1257-to 1507- per kg. in the local market.

Amongst the fishing community it is the Mukhia or Chaibh sub caste which is involved in sweeping the pond floor for collection of seeds (the process is known as Bahariya in local parlance). The Bdanpar or Sahanis perform the task of popping. It needs, expertise at every level, which comes to them from generation to generation.

Since *Makhana* is a cash crop, it is exported from the region to different parts of India and even outside the country. This transportation goes on round the year. The local businessmen store the produce and deal in as per the requirements of the market. The finished product is ready by October. Railways are the chief mode of transport.

References

1. *The Legend of King Ashoka, A study and translation of the Ashokavadana*", John Stron Princeton Library of Asian Translations, 1983.

3

Birth of Sita

Sita (listen meaning "furrow") is the heroine of the epic Ramayana. She is the consort of the god Rama (avatar of Vishnu) and is an avatar of Lakshmi, goddess of wealth and wife of Vishnu. She is esteemed as a standard-setter for wifely and womanly virtues for all Hindu women. Sita is known for her dedication, self-sacrifice, courage and purity. Sita is described as the daughter of the earth goddess Bhûmi and the adopted daughter of King Janaka of Mithila.

Sita is one of the principal figures of the *Ramayana*, a famous Hindu scripture of epic proportions, which details not only the heroic exploits of her husband Lord Rama, but also the sublime love story between Sita and her husband. As the devoted wife of the seventh avatar of Vishnu, Sita is regarded as the most esteemed exemplar of womanly elegance and wifely virtue in Hinduism. She is also considered to be an avatar of Lakshmi, Vishnu's consort, who chose to reincarnate herself on Earth to provide humankind with a paradigmatic example of good virtue. The name Sita is derived from the root 'Sit' whose primary meaning is whiteness-an immaculate and stainless purity. Our Sita lies imprisoned in each of us, tormented by vicious ogresses representing our negative tendencies, much as the heroine of Ramayana is surrounded by wardresses.

She is best known by the name Sita, derived from the Sanskrit word *sîta*, which means furrow. According to Ramayana, Janaka found her while ploughing as a part of a *yagna* and adopted her. The word *sîta* was a poetic term in ancient India, its imagery redolent of fecundity and the many blessings coming from settled agriculture. The Sita of the Ramayana may have been named after a more ancient Vedic goddess Sita, who is mentioned once in the Rigveda as an earth goddess who blesses the land with good crops. In the Vedic era, She was one of the goddesses associated with fertility. A Vedic hymn (Rig Veda 4:57) recites:

"Auspicious Sita, come thou near;

We venerate and worship thee

That thou mayst bless and prosper us

And bring us fruits abundantly."

In *Harivansha* Sita has been invoked as one of the names of goddess Arya:

O goddess, you are the altar's center in the sacrifice,

"The priest's fee

Sita to those who hold the plough

And Earth to all living being."

The *Kausik-sutra* and the *Paraskara-sutra* associate her repeatedly as the wife of *Parjanya* (a god associated with rains) and Indra.

Sita is known by many epithets. She is called *Jânaki* as the daughter of Janaka; *Maithili* as the princess of Mithila. As the wife of Rama, she is called *Ramâ*. Her father Janaka had earned the sobriquet *Videha* due to his ability to transcend body consciousness; Sita is therefore also known as *Vaidehi*.

The Sanskrit word *Sita* literally means "the line made by the plough or furrow," a term held by ancient Indians to be redolent of fecundity and the many blessings that accrue from settled agriculture. Accordingly, the goddess known as Sita appearing in early Vedic literature is closely connected to the earth and is thought to bless the land with good crops. In various texts, Sita is listed as the wife of gods who hold jurisdiction over the fertile rains, such as Parjanya and even Indra. In the *Vajasaneyi-samhita*, Sita is invoked when furrows are drawn during a sacrificial ritual. This Vedic goddess of the fertile earth, though she remains relatively insignificant in these early texts, may represent a prototype of the character Sita who appears in the *Ramayana*. The role of kings in ancient India was often described in terms of promoting fertility of the land over which they ruled. Thus the significance of pairing Rama (the archetypal ruler) with a wife connected to the earth's bounty was readily apparent.

Sita's origin has been the subject of scholarly studies. Sita's birth and parentage have been depicted differently in different versions of Ramayana.

§ **Valmiki's Ramayana:** In Valmiki's Ramayana and Kamban's Tamil epic Iramavataram, Sita is said to have discovered in a furrow in a ploughed field, and for that reason is regarded as a daughter of Bhûmi Devi (the goddess earth). She was discovered, adopted and brought up by Janaka, king of Mithila, and his wife Sunayana.

§ **Ramayana Manjari:** In *Ramayana Manjari* (verses 344–366), North-western and Bengal recensions of Valmiki Ramayana, it has been described as on hearing a voice from the sky and then seeing Menaka, Janaka expresses his wish to obtain a child. And when he finds the child, he hears the same voice again telling him the infant is his spiritual child, born of Menaka.

§ **Janka's real Daughter:** In *Ramopkhyana* of the Mahabharata and also in *Paumachariya* of Vimala Suri, Sita has been depicted as Janaka's real daughter. According to Rev. Fr. C. Bulcke, this motif that Sita was the real daughter of Janaka, as described in *Ramopkhyana Mahabharata* was based on the authentic version of *Valmiki Ramayana*. Later the story of Sita miraculously appearing in furrow was inserted in *Valmiki Ramayana*.

§ **Reincarnation of Vedavati:** Some versions of the *Ramayana* suggest that Sita was a reincarnation of Vedavati. Ravana tried to molest Vedavati and her chastity was sullied beyond Ravana's redemption when she was performing penance to become consort of Vishnu. Vedavati immolated herself on a pyre to escape Ravana's lust, vowing to return in another age and be the cause of Ravana's destruction. She was duly reborn as Sita.

Sita was *ayonija*, not born of anyone womb. Rama, the seventh Avatar of Vishnu in the Hindu tradition. Sita is one of the principal characters in the Ramayana. Sita was a foundling, discovered in a furrow in a ploughed field, and for that reason is regarded as a daughter of Bhumi Devi, the goddess of the Earth. She was found and adopted by Janaka, king of Mithila, now in state of Bihar and his wife Sunayana. She is esteemed as the standard setter for wifely and womanly virtues for all Hindu women. Understood theologically in Hinduism, Sita is an Avatar of Lakshmi.

Some versions of the Ramayana suggest that Sita was a reincarnation of Vedavati (an avatar of Lakshmi), an orphan lady. Sita as Daughter of Ravana-The Story of Sita Born as Daughter of Ravana. There is an interesting story mentioned in some books and folk tales that mentions Sita as the daughter of Ravana. Legend has it that Vedavati, a pious woman, wanted to marry Srihari Vishnu. To marry Vishnu, she gave up worldly life and became a hermit and built an ashram on a riverbank.

Once while Vedavati was meditating on the riverbank, Ravana, the demon king, happened to see her. He was enamored by her beauty and tried to violate her. To escape from Ravana she jumped into a fire pit created for *yajna*. Before dying she cursed Ravana that in her next birth she will be responsible for his death. In her next birth, Vedavati was born as Ravana's daughter. Soon after she was born, a voice from the sky warned that the baby will be responsible for her father's death. To save his life, Ravana threw the little girl child into the sea. The child fell on the lap of sea-goddess Varuni. Goddess Varuni took the girl child to the shores and gave her to earth-goddess Pirthvi. Goddess Prithvi then gave her to King Janaka. As per Ramayana, Sita was found by King Janaka while ploughing a field.

§ **Reincarnation of Manivati**: According to Gunabhadra's *Uttara Purana* of the ninth century BCE, Ravana disturbs asceticism of Manivati, daughter of Amitavega of Alkapuri, and she pledges to take revenge on Ravana. Manivati is later reborn as the daughter of Ravana and Mandodari. But, astrologers predict ruin of Ravana because of this child. So, Ravana orders to kill the child. Manivati is placed in a casket and buried in the ground of Mithila where she is discovered by some of the farmers of the kingdom. Then Janka, king of that state adopts her.

§ **Ravana's Daughter:** In Sanghadasa's Jaina version of Ramayana of the 5th century BCE, Sita, entitled *Vasudevahindi*, is born as daughter of Ravana. According to this version, astrologers predict that first child of Vidyadhara Maya (Ravana's wife) will destroy his lineage. That's why Ravana abandons her and orders the infant to be buried in a distant land where she is later discovered and adopted by Janaka.

Adoption is a legal process that creates a new, permanent parent-child relationship where one didn't exist before. Adoption bestows on the adoptive parent(s) all the rights and responsibilities of a legal parent, and gives the child being adopted all the social, emotional, and legal rights and responsibilities of a family member. Sometimes, will include the words "as if born to" to describe the new parent-child relationship.

In the Roman Empire, adoption was the most common way of acceding to the throne without use of force. The second emperor, Tiberius, was the adopted son of Augustus, beginning general tradition that the Emperor would adopt a successor. During the Roman Empire's first 200 years, this tradition was common with Tiberius, Caligula, Nero, Trajan, Hadrian, Antoninus Pius and Lucius Verus all becoming Emperor through adoption.

Adoption is ancient arrangement. It is spoken of in the Bible. Greeks and Romans, Egyptians and Babylonians all had adoption systems. Adoption is the process whereby parents are supplied for parent-less children or for those children whose parents are unable to provide for their care. It also provides children for childless couples, or in modern society for childless individuals as well.

Sita, Rama's wife, the adopted daughter of King Janaka. Sita was found in the furrows of a sacred field, and was regarded by the people of Janaka's kingdom as a blessed child. Sita is born in the kingdom of Videha. Her birth was a mystery from the beginning. It was said that she was found in a container in the form of an egg on a furrow, on a day when King Janaka was doing some work in the field. This mysterious birth seems to have deep significance, Sita being thus born by the Mother Earth from an egg that signify any future creation. King Janaka took the 'daughter of the Earth' with him and rose her as his own daughter.

Since childhood Sita received a good education. She liked to sing, thus king Janaka arranged to train her in playing musical instruments. Her voice was sweet, her presence was lovely and enchanting. People around loved her very much. Her musical skills were so proficient that other versions of Ramayana beside Valmiki's, described her as being a Gandharva girl, a heavenly musical virtuoso. Thus her skills and abilities were able to match the best Gandharvas in heaven. But Sita was much more, as Valmiki and later on Tulsidasa in his devotional Ramayana known as Ramacharitamanasa has written.

After many years, the time for Sita's marriage has arrived and king Janaka knowing that something unusual was about his adopted daughter, has decided to marry her only with an unusual man. Thus he setup a contest involving Shiva's bow, a mighty weapon that was seen as impossible to be used by any mortal. King Janaka was convinced that his daughter has divine origin and only a man of similar extraction could marry her.

Enigmatic Sita and her Enigmatic Birth

In a book of O'Flaherty, Wendy D. Textual Sources for the Study of Hinduism. Pub: University of Chicago Press. p. 59, Ramayana 1:65, Devanagari manuscript w-1455,' it is written that: "[Janaka:] 'Now, one day when I was in the sacrificial grounds, I saw the ultimate celestial nymph, Menaka, flying through the sky, and this thought came to me: 'If I should have a child in her, what a child that would be!' As I was thinking in this way, my semen fell on the ground. And afterwards, as I was ploughing that field, there arose out of the earth, as first fruits, my daughter, who has celestial beauty and qualities, and can only be won by one whose bride price is his manliness. Since she arose from the surface of the earth, and was born from no womb, she is called Sita, the furrow.'"

Sita is considered to be the nature's nature, Primordeal Nature, Mahaa Prakriti, and when the five elements of nature intermingle into one, that is the Manifest Nature, where the five elements are *pridhvi, aapa, teja, vaayu, aakaasha* 'earth, waters, fire, air and space...' and there are many theories of their commingling like, *pachii karana, saptii karana* quintuplication, and sevenfold commingling etc. The process of creation gives rise to 24 items: 1] empirical or fundamental matter, 2] *mahat*, 3] *ahamkaara*, 4-8] five subtle elements, 9-13] five gross elements, 14] mind, 15-19] five sense organs, 20-24] five motor organs, 25] *jiiva aatma*, individual's soul, 26] Brahman, The Absolute. With these, a created living being is created. This is in the case of mortals and their births. But when Sita is found in the furrow all these things have already happened and there is no question of human pregnancy to be attached to her. Hence Sita is to be taken as Goddess Lakshmi, who is *paraa shakti*, Vishnu *Maya* and when she has to take an incarnation to become the prime cause to the effect of eliminating Ravana, no human activity of reproduction can be attached to such beings. If she were to be a human, perhaps she would not have exited from the pyre of fire when she self-immolated, after Rama and Ravana war. Some more information, though unrelated to Valmiki Ramayana, is given hereunder.

lakÿmym kÿyra samudra raja tanayam sryranga dhmeþvarym|

dasy bhta samasta deva vanitm lokaika dypa ankurm ||

Lakshmi evolved from the Milky Ocean, when gods and demons churned it for amrita, the Divine Elixir, along with it a host of other items like, *haalaahala*, [cosmic poison,] *candra* Moon, *kalpa vriksha*, [Benevolent Divine Tree,] and the medicinal sage-god Dhanvantari holding the golden pot of amrita, have come out as has been explained by Vishvamitra to Rama in this *Kanda*.

Vishnu is the all-inclusive deity, known as *purusha* or *mahaa puruSa... parama aatma* Supreme Person, *naraayaNa* one who peregrinates mortals in and out this mortal world, *antaryämi* The In-dweller of all beings, and He is the *shèshin* the Totality, in whom all souls are contained. He is bhagavat where *bhaga*, derives from the root *bhaj* meaning Gracious Lord, and vat one who has it. Vishnu possesses six such divine glories *Sadguna vibhuuti*, namely, 1] *jnaana*, Omniscience 2] *aishwarya*, Providence, 3] *shakti*, Omnicompetence, 4] *bala*, Omnipotence, 5] *viirya*, Immutability. 6] *tèjas*, Resplendence, *shakti* is the *samvit*, the Primary Intelligence of God, while the other five attributes emerge from this *samvid* and hence *shakti* is the god's *ahámata* Personality and Activity. Thus this *Shakti* of god is personified in mythological lore and is called *Shri* or Lakshmi, and She is said to manifest herself in, 1] *kriyaa shakti*,

Creative Activity and 2] *bhuuti shakti*, Creation of God. Hence Vishnu cannot part with His own personality or creativity i.e., *ahamta*, which in its feminine form is called *shri* or Lakshmi. He therefore needs His consort Goddess Lakshmi to be with Him always, untouched by any. Thus, Goddess Lakshmi has to accompany Vishnu in all His incarnations, along with other paraphernalia like his conch-shell, his quoit and mace, and the thousand headed serpent *aadi shesa* etc. Such a delightful deity Goddess Lakshmi is a treasure house that can be abducted by the greedy, but she is fickle like ripples *lakÿmy hi toya taranga capal Lakshmi= Goddess Lakshmi; hi= indeed; toya= water; taranga= wave like; capalaa=* wavering. 'Goddess Lakshmi is wavering like the waves of water...' *chapala, chanchala, asthira*, wavering, faltering, unstable, and *maayaa, maa + yaa* 'whose illusory play she is, or *liila* play of god. She comes in unnoticeably like the water in a coconut and evaporates innocently into thin air, at Her will. Such as she is she is easily grabbed by the greedy. Hence none can give birth to her except the Mother Nature, and hence she is called *mahilaa* ; *mahi + laa* where *mahi* is earth and *laa lah khandane trisu aadaane stri* because Mother Earth gave birth to Sita, Sita is *mahila.* Hence it is better to avoid assuming her to be an ordinary lady of an ordinary birth, and she may be viewed either legendarily or mythologically, for Valmiki as an epical poet, himself has not chronicled the details of her birth.

Even Vishnu is deprived of Her in His incarnations, not only in Ramayana but also in His *narsimha* Man-Lion incarnation. There, Maya Lakshmi becomes a tribal woman to bring back the ferocious Lion-Man to his original form. And in other versions of Ramayana, it is said that Ravana abducted Maya Sita, but not real Sita. 'When the real Sita herself is an enigma, what if Ravana abducts real or duplicate copy of that Sita...' is the brushed aside adjustment. In either case, it is *maya, liila* illusory power, sport of Vishnu together with that of Goddess Lakshmi, cause this enigma. Hence, whenever She is thus absconding from Him, Vishnu searches and retrieves Her, for no one in Universe can handle her, nor amass all the wealth. The predestined wealth alone is enjoyable but nothing more can be amassed. So also are the riches in the present day world, come too suddenly and vanish that suddenly. No one is rich ever and anon, and on someday everyone is likely to see the ups and downs in his graph of riches. It is Vishnu that retrives the real wealth back to His abode *Vaikuntha*, and even punishes anyone for his accumulation of beyond-the-means-wealth. The burning of Lanka by Hanumana in Sundara Kanda is an example to this.

In Lakshmi tantra, a Vaishnavaite *aagama* text, She that unrestrainable Goddess Lakshmi declares Herself, as *naaraayanii, vaisnavii i.e., a coequal of Vishnu, in the play of the universe i.e., in God's liila, saying that: aham narayany nama sa satta vaiÿõavy para* 'I am indeed *naaraayanii* i.e. Lakshmi, the Supreme Essence of Vishnu... [Lakshmi Tantra 3.1.]

The Hindu mythology bases more on its eighteen Puraanas, each of the six is rendered to each of the Hindu Trinity, Brahma, Vishnu, and Shiva. A] Vishnu Puraanas are: 1] Vishnu, 2] bhaagavata, 3] naaradiiya, 4] garuda, 5] Padma, 6] varaaha, B] Brahma Puraana, - 1] Brahma, 2] brahmaanda, 3] brahmavaivarta, 4] maarkandèya, 5] bhavisya, 6] vaamana, C] Shiva Puraana, 1] vaayu, 2] linga, 3] skanda, 4] agni, 5] matsya, 6] kurma. In all these Puraana-s Goddess Lakshmi is given a laudable place without any sectarian dispute. In the Vaishnavaite Puraana-s, Shiva starts telling the efficacy of Vishnu to Goddess Parvati. While Shaiva mythology places Goddess Parvati, the consort of Shiva, in one half of Shiva's body *ardha naariishvara tattva*, and Vaishnavaite tradition places Goddess Lakshmi in the heart of Vishnu itself, as if it is a Lotus hridaya kamala. This is to depict the inseparable unison of Universal *purusha*, Male and *prakriti* , Female, the seed and field.

While Valmiki Ramayana names Rama as Rama, the Padma Puraana etc., mythological texts bring in the Vedic texts and prefix *shrii* of shrii suukta of Rig Veda khila 5-87, which is a feminine counterpart of *purusa sukta* of Rig Veda 10-90, for *parama purusha* i.e., Vishnu or Narayana, and thus call Rama of Valmiki as *shrii* raama. Vaishnavaite mythologies take hold of these and other Vedic references to Vishnu, and treat Vishnu/Narayana and Lakshmi as the inseparable divine couple, who maintain this Universe. The prefix *shrii* means as 'one who takes delight in *shrii* i.e., Lakshmi, meaning wealth, wealth of any kind. *shrii riti prathamam naama lakshmyaa* and' if a is the first name of Vishnu, *shrii* is the first name of Lakshmi. Thus, primarily eight kinds of wealth are established, to be associated with Goddess Lakshmi. They are 1] *aadi Lakshmi* Wealth a priori 2] *dhaanya Lakshmi* Cereal Wealth 3] *Dhairya Lakshmi* Wealth of Courage 4] *gaja Laksmi* Elephant Wealth, i.e., Elephantine Wealth of all animals and livestock, *santaana Lakshmi* Wealth of Progeny, 6] *vijaya Lakshmi*, Wealth of Victory, 7] *vidyaa Lakshmi* Wealth of Education, 8] *dhana Lakshmi* Monetary Wealth. And anything that need be affluent gets the auspicious prefix *shrii* or suffix lakshmi, and called *raajya Lakshmi*, Wealth of Empire, *bhaagya lakshmi* Wealth of Fortune, and the like...

The play of Goddess Lakshmi in the form of Sita is Ramayana. As such, her absence from Rama caused Rama to travel up to Lanka, annihilate the evil, and retrieve her. Sita herself expresses her anguish about Rama's indulgence in a Supreme welfare-state, than in herself, as *Mahaakavi* Kalidasa, in his epical poem Raghu Vamsha, and depicts what this *bhaagya* lakshmi has to say, when Rama, basing on some satirical remarks of his lowly subject, deserts Sita in favour of *raajya* lakshmi when Sita said as below:

upasthitm prvam apsya lakymym vanam may srthamasi prapanna |

tadaspadam prpya tayti royt soyh asmi na tad bhavane vasanty ||
raghuvamsha

"Earlier you refused the kingdom-wealth, *raajya lakshmi* and came to forests, where I was with you. Now that, that kingdom-wealth, *raajya lakshmi* on winning your affection is jealous of me, who am your *bhaagya lakshmi* 'fortune-wealth...' and she does not let me live in your palace." And thus, Sita departs Rama to forests, at the fag end of Ramayana.

Valmiki declares Ramayana is *siithaayaah charitam mahaan...* 'Sita's impeccable conduct...' by giving her an unusual birth from the furrow of the plough, and in the end she exits from this world into the same soil, where the earth is called *vasundhara*, which cleaves under Sita's feet, and takes Sita into her womb again. As such, the reason for Sita to be there in that furrow as baby is said to be a vow of Goddess Lakshmi, in her earlier incarnation as Vedavati. The mythologies go on to say that Vedavati is the brainchild of a sage called Kushadhwaja, and he decides to give Vedavati in marriage none less than Vishnu. But in his lifetime, it is an unfulfilled desire. Then Vedavati starts a rigorous penance to achieve her father's wish. When she is at her culmination point of her penance, Ravana, passing that way in sky sees this beautiful lady, nears, and disturbs her penance. Vedavati coming out of her meditation, curses Ravana saying that she will reincarnate herself, to destroy Ravana and his entire dynasty. Then she causes a yogic fire and immolates herself in it. And Vedavati is reborn as Sita of Ramayana, in an unusual way.

Here *aananda raamaayana* has an interesting parable. Once there was a king named Padmaaksha who wanted Lakshmi as his daughter. On practising ascesis Vishnu appears and gives a fruit called *maatulunga phala*, and girl emerges from out of that fruit, and she is named as Padma. But greedy to possess her, all the wooing kings war with *Padmaaksha* and his entire family is ruined and Padma jumps into fire and self immolates herself. Later when Vishnu's *maaya* comes out of an altar of fire, sits in her meditation, Ravana sees her and wants to abduct her. Of course, she is otherwise said to be Vedavati in other texts. But again, she enters the fire altar and reduces herself to ashes. Even then, Ravana searches in those ashes for her. In there, he gets five diamonds of high quality. He comes to Lanka and places those diamonds in a casket and jovially presents them to his wife Mandodari. When Mandodari could not lift the casket Ravana lifts it and opens its lid, as he lifted Mt. Kailash. When the casket is opened, Mandodari finds a baby girl in it and recognises her to be Goddess Lakshmi. Then they consult their teachers about that baby's arrival. Those teaches wishing good for Ravana, advise to get rid off this girl immediately, for he is Goddess Lakshmi, arrived here only to end Ravana and his dynasty. Then Mandodari orders his servants to carry away this baby in a casket by an aircraft and get rid off it.

But Ravana rushes after the girl with a sword, to put that girl to sword. Empress Mandodari pacifies Ravana and says "Why purchase a later time death now itself at the hand of this baby... let that the casket be buried..." Ravana agrees. Mandodari also curses this girl saying, "this faithless girl, [for wealth is unfaithful,] will thrive only in a house, where the householder has his senses conquered, and who being an emperor lives like a perfect hermit, and who though wealthy and supreme by himself, will care nothing for the riches but view whole of the world and people as his own soul, with an impartial attitude..." Thus this casket is buried in the fields of King Janaka's empire by demons, clandestinely. Mandodari thought that such a person is an impossibility to take birth in this mortal world, to foster this buried girl, and thus presumed her curse to be twisty. But there is King Janaka with all the above attributes. A king without ego, wealthy but living simple, childless, yet does not crave for one, like King Dasharatha. Hence, he is called *raajarsi* a saintly king. Sita's birth is to be limitedly understood, as said by Janaka in this chapter. Otherwise, the nuances about the birth of Sita are to be viewed through the viewfinders of mythologies, legends, and above all, through the viewfinders of tradition... but not in the vast of epical poetry, as Valmiki himself has undocumented it...

4

The Beauty of Beauty

Beauty is a package that goes beyond the physical to connect you to your deep inner self. The feeling goes beyond the squeaky cleanliness that a good grooming session gives one. This is not just about physical appearance, but about a strange and beautiful connection with the inner self, a spurt of confidence, and a feeling of empowerment. Whenever you do anything to make yourself look or feel better exercising, eating healthy, beauty treatments or relaxation therapies–you are left with a level of confidence and a sense of rightness that is difficult to replicate. So it is not just vanity that drives people to strive to be their most beautiful selves. but an inner urge to feel powerful and spiritually connected to one's own self. And that is the real power of beauty that it goes far deeper than mere looks. Think of any person you consider beautiful. Is it just the arrangement of their features, the texture of their skin, sheen of their hair or the structure of their bodies that make them beautiful to you? Do you not think of the goodness that shines through their eyes, their warmth and generosity of spirit? Does not a sense of humility intensify beauty? In order to be effective and meaningful, beauty needs to go beyond the physical.

Do beautiful and well-groomed people have an advantage over others? They definitely do! Easier on the eye, they attract attention more easily, are perceived to be above average in everything they do, and work their way out of situations with greater ease. They find it easier to clinch jobs and good partners. A sloppy person gives the impression of someone who is not in control of his or her life whereas a well-groomed person looks capable of moving mountains!

Once we understand that beauty is an entire package of which good looks is just one part, it is easier to accept that each and everyone of us can be beautiful and great lookers. It is just a question of working on one's advantages, being well-groomed always, eating healthy and exercising, cultivating a generous and caring spirit, and projecting oodles of confidence. And this holds true of both men and women. Who says men don't need to be beautiful? Of course, they do!

Beauty is about individuality. There is nothing more beautiful than a woman Who values uniqueness. Beauty is somebody's inner self. A beautiful person is someone with kindness and happiness, a good spirit and a good soul. Think of Cinderella or Pygmalion -both stories where ordinary girls get transformed into beauties. Both these tales are as much about inner as outward beauty. Both Cinderella and Eliza Doolittle are women of substance who are compassionate and humble. Pantaloons Femina Miss India Vanya Mishra who won the 'Beauty with a Purpose' title at Miss World 2012 recently, talks of how being beautiful is about service beyond one's self. She also concurs that grooming helps "bring out positivity and absorb the negativity".

Scott Barnes, top make-up artist to celebrities from Jennifer Lopez to Gwyneth Paltrow, confesses that when he looks at women, he finds each and every one of them beautiful as "each one is distinct". In his book, About Face, he says, "Beauty is not about looking like everybody else, but finding your own uniqueness, knowing what sets you apart and accepting yourself-the parts you love and those you don't and then working with all of it."

To call anything beautiful is always the highest form of aesthetic praise. Indeed, if ethics is an investigation into what constitutes goodness, than aesthetics is an enquiry into the nature of the beautiful. The most comprehensive lexicon of the Sanskrit Language, the '*Shabda Kalpadrum*,' defines the word '*sundara*' (beauty), as a perception which makes the heart melt (*ardra*). In this context, consider the portrait of Sita painted by the poet in the middle of the *sundar-kanda*, a poignant and moving picture of a helpless creature in trying and painful circumstances.

She sits desolate on the bare ground, pale, emaciated, her body soiled and her spirit worn down by grief, the very image of an inner beauty dimmed by outward circumstance. The poet is so moved at her monumental suffering that he lets forth a shower of similes and metaphors describing her condition, representing one of the finest aesthetic moments in the entire epic:

'Sita seemed to scorch the nearby vegetation with her deep sighs. Her beauty, now only faintly discernible, resembled a fire clouded by smoke. She was clad in a single yellow garment, resembling a pond without lotuses. Abashed and disconsolate, she was like the dove cut off from her herd and surrounded by a pack of hounds. Her hair was formed into a single braid (*ek-veni*), falling like a black serpent on her back. Seated on the ground like a branch fallen from a tree, she resembled a blurred memory or a fortune lost, a faith betrayed or a hope dashed, like a reputation lost due to false rumor.'

'Looking here and there like a delicate fawn, Sita was barely discernible, like a Vedic text once learned by heart but now nearly lost through the lack of recitation. It was only with great difficulty that Hanumana was able to recognize her, because she was like a word whose meaning has changed due to inapt usage. Even then, keeping her faith, the firm lady looked no more agitated than the river Ganga, which however heavy the rainfall, never floods.'

'Weighed down by grief, Sita was like a ship at sea burdened by heavy cargo. She resembled a star, whose positive *karma* now exhausted, had fallen down from heaven to the earth. Lacking in all ornaments, she was adorned only by the love for her husband. In the absence of her lord, she was rendered mute like an untouched *vina*.'

'Her body was covered with dirt, however, she was adorned with her own physical beauty, thus, like a tender lotus stalk covered with mud she both lacked beauty and possessed it. She seemed to be a wave risen from the ocean of grief. Like a command disobeyed, or the skies aflame at the time of a catastrophe, she was like a river run dry. She resembled a pond ruined by elephants, its lotus blossoms and leaves torn up and the birds frightened away. This was the condition of Sita, like a little girl abandoned in the midst of desolate wilderness.'

Thus we observe that the poet has poured out his heart's content in describing Sita's condition in her confinement. This is not surprising. Earlier he dedicates the whole of Ramayana to her, naming it 'The Great Saga of Sita' (*sitayas charitam mahat*). (Ramayana, 1.4.7)

Many scholars feel the *sundara-kanda* to be an epic in its own right, and go even as far as to suggest that it was only to highlight it that Valmiki composed the remaining portions of the Ramayana. The central theme of *sundara-kanda* is the noble character of Sita, brightened all the more in adversity, even as gold when heated shines in even greater splendor.

Indeed, whose heart would not melt and flow in a stream of devotion towards this sensitive portrayal of one of the most venerated figures in Indian thought? It was Mahatma Gandhi who said "true beauty is that which consists of a purity of heart." In this respect perhaps, the character of Sita, as developed in the *sundara-kanda*, is unparalleled in the annals of world literature, portraying her as a woman chaste in both thought and deed, ever graceful in her sorrow.

Beauty: Going Beyond the Physical

This description however, puts focus only on the physical, and rightly so, for the physical sphere is the locus of the manifestation of internal qualities. Nevertheless, true beauty does not merely stimulate the aesthetic senses; it also kindles the imagination, presenting first to the view only the broad outline of a picture, which has to be then completed in all necessary details by the imaginative power of the aesthete. According to the Indian philosopher Abhinavagupta, aesthetic experience is not static, but dynamic. It has inexhaustible potentialities, which appear to be new at every moment to the onlooker.

This is one area where the Ramayana abounds in plenty. Thus even the small fact of Sita keeping a single serpentine braid is pregnant with meaning. Keeping her hair open makes a woman look all the more attractive and thus tying it up in a single strand was the only practical thing to do. That women, when hard pressed for time, unable to do any makeup, just quickly tie up their tresses in a single strand, retaining both modesty and utility. Additionally, Sita's braid is like a serpent, making it clear that it would be fatal for a man (except her husband) to touch her.

The imaginative streak of the reader runs further riot when Ravana comes to confront Sita in the garden, the whole episode being watched over by Hanumana. As Satan asks the virtuous lady to accept his indecent proposal, she answers him befittingly, but not before she has placed a blade of grass between herself and the demon. Ancient commentators have waxed eloquent on why Sita placed this straw:

a) The straw, acting as a symbolic purdah, highlighted the ideal of purity which deterred a woman from holding face-to-face conversation with a man other than her husband.

b) She pointed out to Ravana that she considered him to be of no more consequence than a blade of grass.

c) Sita said symbolically: "Since you are like a beast, here is some fodder for you."

d) Once during their exile in the forest, a crow had pestered Sita, targeting her with his beak. Angered at its arrogance, Rama had picked up a blade of grass and thrown it like a missile at the crow, blinding the bird. Sita is thus pointing out to Ravana that just as the lord punished the crow with a mere twig so will you be destroyed.

e) Ravana's cowardly behavior in kidnapping Sita saturated his sins, and his destruction was but now inevitable, making it the last straw to break the camel's back.

In the mansion of beauty, there are several layers, and what is outwardly apparent is the least important. The palpably beautiful exterior becomes worthy of notice only to the extent it serves as an appropriate medium for the inner beauty core, which constitutes the soul or essence of poetry. We have seen above that at the center of beauty is situated Sita, however, Hanumana's quest is suggestive of a much deeper symbolism than a mere search for the 'physical' Sita.

Tulsidas says on Sita:

Beauty beautiful does she make,

A lamp shining in charm's wake.

(Ramacharitmanas of Tulsidas, 1.230.4)

Sita is thus the concentrated essence of all beauty in this world, and in his search, Hanumana is in fact looking for the essential spiritual core of all that is beautiful in the universe. In Tulsidas' version, the chapter of beauty begins with Hanumana climbing up a high mountain, using it as a prop to leap across the mighty ocean to the city of Lanka where Sita is imprisoned:

Here it must be stressed that this crass attempt at rendering Tulsidas' sublime verses in English is nowhere near the original since 'poetry is what gets lost in translation.'

In the symbolic world of Tulsidas, Sita is but the embodied form of *bhakti*, the essential characteristics of which are complete faith and total surrender, all of which find their culmination in her. *Bhakti* is not the mere waving of ornamental lamps in front of the image of a deity; rather, it is a way of life. The *Narada Bhakti Sutras*, an ancient text laying down the philosophical foundations of *bhakti*, says:

Bhakti is of the nature of a result (to be achieved). (*Sutra* 26)

Bhakti thus is not a path, but the goal of life, and the "beautiful" mountain represents the spiritual heights which have to be gained before making this mighty leap across the massive sea of ego before we find it.

Mother and Son

In order to win over Sita's faith, Hanumana has to first present his credentials as an authorized emissary of god. Before starting off, he had been given a ring by Rama, encrusted with the latter's name, to be presented to Sita. Seeing an opportune moment, Hanumana drops it into her hands:

Here we find another instance of the word beautiful. The poet is pointing out to us that it is the divine name of god (and its chanting), which introduces us to *bhakti*, helping us to establish a fruitful relationship; and what indeed is the nature of this relationship? Tulsidas says:

Janaki, mother of world, Janak's offspring.

Dearest to Rama of compassionate bearing.

Her two lotus feet i do propitiate,

A spotless intellect is her grace.

(Ramacharitmanas, 1.18.4)

When we identify ourselves merely with our "body", our kinship is limited only to our own immediate family. However, if we wish to identify ourselves with a universal family, and reach out to the one *Maha Shakti* who is the mother of all, we will need to cross over the restraining ocean of ego.

As a matter of fact, it is in the *sundara-kanda* that Sita first addresses Hanumana as her son; and what is the first thing he asks for from his mother?

Food.

Hanumana knows very well that this is a sure shot way of kindling motherly affection. Truly, the supreme feminine emotion is to nourish her children, superseding all other feelings. It is mentioned in the Bhagavata Purana that the very thought of her adorable Krishna coming back home in the evening makes milk ooze out of mother Yashoda's breasts. In the modern world, this is exemplified in the venerable institution called the 'Jewish mother,' much celebrated in humor.

Rama's mother Kaushalya too is equally "Jewish". She has just been informed that her son will be crowned as king tomorrow, and this is what she says to him:

Go fast my dear son a bath do take,

A sweet of your choice then partake.

(Ramacharitmanas, 2.53.1)

A father is happy to see his son crowned. A mother gets all the happiness in the world when his belly is (over) full.

Sita, while giving permission to Hanumana to eat, is more philosophical about it:

"Go dear, and enjoy the soft and sweet fruits, dedicating your heart to the feet of Lord Rama." (Ramacharitmanas, 5.17)

Indeed, this but echoes the vision of the Bhagavad Gita where all fruits are rendered sweet when first offered to god.

Beauty in Ugliness

In this metaphorical universe, no aspect is what it seems at the first sight. All that is presented to the view is suggestive of a deeper essence. Thus Sita imprisoned in the golden city of Lanka is our own essential core, always in connection with the supreme reality. The Isha Upanishad says:

'The face of truth is covered with a golden vessel. Uncover it, O god, that I who am truth itself may see it.' (*Mantra* 15)

The monkey Hanumana is none other our own restless mind, hopping from one desire (branch) to another. Further, a monkey is often the butt of ridicule, and calling someone as having a "monkey face," is perhaps an ultimate expression of ugliness. Yet, it is such a creature who discovers the truest manifestation of beauty, and in the process, becomes beautiful himself. This is subtle message of the *sundara-kanda*, that we have to find beauty amongst all the negativity of life, whether it be the rich golden city of Lanka standing on a foundation of deceit and lust, surrounded by ugly ogresses, and confined by our excessive attachment to physical beauty (Ravana).

The *sundara-kanda* is beautiful because it belongs to *sundari* Sita. Not only is she the essence of all that is truly beautiful in the world, she is the powerful medium to which even Rama has to take recourse to in order to express his own divine beauty.

In the Valmiki Ramayana Sita says:

"I am as inseparable from Rama as radiance is from the sun." (5.21.15)

The implication being that Rama is as dependent on Sita as she on him. He is but the formless supreme reality unable to make itself available to human perception. It is only the devoted *shakti* of *bhakti* which grants *Nirguna* both the motivation and the capability to express itself as *Saguna*.

Spiritual Beauty of Sita

All living creatures, Creation has two aspects; '*para*', the subtle, foundational aspect and '*a-para*,' the sensory aspect.

The five elements, earth, water, fire, air and space along with mind, intellect and ego constitute the eight '*a-para*' or senory aspects which are personified as the Sita who represents the *para* aspect in an individual, which is *prana shakti* or life force, divine power that brings to life the individual soul.

Just as subatomic, intermolecular and inter-galactic space are indivisible parts of the same space, the *prana shakti* that is being referred to is inseparable from chaitanya, the same all-pervading power.

It is the experiential realisation of the Self that we really yearn for and even attain, by '*aradhana*', which means inner worship.

That to which or whom we owe our existence is our Lord. Naturally then, the pervading '*chaitanya*', personified as Sri Rama, is the Lord of all creation. Sita adore the benevolence of the Lord and by way of worship, surrender absolutely and unconditionally to this power. This they do with an inner attitude that a devoted spouse has for her partner, that of her companion being the sole one in whom her soul is anchored and without whom, she is a mere corpse.

Sita is the personification of any individual soul creature, whose sustenance is done by the same universal *chaitanya*. It is *chaitanya* that runs through all the sense organs and makes them perform their various functions. The organs certainly do not have their own separate power.

In yoga parlance, it means that in order to experience the presence and benevolence of the of the presence and benevolence of the all pervading Divinity, we too must awaken or invoke the latent divine power, known as *Kundalini*, the Goddess who is dormant at the physical sphere of human awareness.

Once awakened, the *Kundalini* enables inner purification by means of a process of various yoga-*kriyas* that are autonomous to *Kundalini*. By leading a life as outlined by one's guru, the *Kundalini* rapidly moves up the body to enable the individual's realisation of Sri Rama, who is the all-prevading *chaitanya*. After this, there is no sorrow, no hate and no fear. One is free, this state of freedom from all attachment is what is described as an intrinsic part of the enlightened state, a state of equanimity and realisation.

There are five aspects of spirituality-the objective, "the why of spirituality, the means for attaining the objective, who pursues spirituality and when."

Objective of spirituality is to transcend the limited bodily identity and experience the oneness of the single whole that this creation is.

'Why should, or rather, why does, one pursue spirituality? We can start by saying that one gets a desire to pursue spirituality and hence goes ahead with it. Then comes the question, why does one person get that desire and why don't thousands of others get it? The only answer to this question can be that the Creator wants it that way.

The means of attaining the objective can vary from one person to another. But they must essentially serve the purpose of transcending the physical world. And physical world and our bodily identity are two sides of the same coin. Many tend to argue that spirituality cannot be divorced from worldly living as spirituality basically entails living normally, albeit with an attitude that I am something more than the physical body. While this may make sense to most spiritual seekers, there is a danger that it will amount to nothing more than hypocrisy. One may continue to merrily indulge in worldly pursuits and simply keep telling himself now and then that there is a soul beyond the body.' That will be self-deception. It is unlikely to bring any spiritual experiences to such a person.

Many believe that spirituality means living in a noble way by practising honesty, integrity, charity, selflessness and other such noble qualities. These are, no doubt, an important preparation towards attaining the ultimate objective. Such '*satkarmas*' lead to accumulation of *shuddha punya*, credit for good deeds. However, this is not the be-all-end-all of spirituality for it would confuse means with the end. If one falls into that trap, when, in fact, one wants to reach a destination! Yes, he will get the side benefit. But he won't be progressing towards the ultimate goal. Without *vairagya* or detachment, it might not lead to the ultimate goal of Self-realisation.

Now about the who part. *Satkarmas* leading to accumulation of *shuddha punya* are like a walk towards the gate to the ultimate destination. However, for the ultimate experience, one has to enter the other side through the gate. Now, it is here an element of divine grace is required. The reason to bring in the aspect of divine grace is because how the selection is made is not known to us, nor can it be understood. That is why even Jesus Christ said that the gate is narrow and many will jostle to enter; but only a few will manage to get in. However, a seeker desirous of attaining the ultimate goal must put in his best efforts. That is the only thing within his capacity.

When does one go on to the spiritual path? It may depend on many complex factors, it including past *karma*. So, an easy answer would be that it depends on the sovereign plan of the Creator.

Spiritual experiences cannot be had through one or more of our five bodily senses. They are the kind that can be perceived directly from inside in one's consciousness. For this to be possible, one has to have a really intense desire for it. He has to switch the physical world off completely for as long as possible. Only then can he make himself eligible for receiving spiritual experience.

Some people are simply born with a happiness gene. They lead a happy life irrespective of their circumstances whether they (are materially successful or not; marry a loving partner or not; are healthy or ailing. The rest of, us instinctively drift towards experiencing incompleteness, sadness and anxiety, as if we carry a dominant unhappiness gene within us.

Coined as an acronym 'MOODS', here are five key symptoms of our unhappiness gene. Understanding these can be greatly helpful in working through our moments of anxiety and depression.

'Me' represents our self-centered instincts to take things personally. We are quick to judge our successes and failures, compliments and critique, and take them personally. Every Untoward incident raises the question of 'why is it happening to me?' Happiness lies in grasping the laws of nature and acknowledging that life is unfolding as it needs to and that every change in our circumstances is not a reflection of us. Also, nothing is happening uniquely to us every one has their share of challenges; it's how we react to them that makes the real difference.

Overwhelmed: Next is our tendency to get totally consumed by unpleasant events. Feeling anxious, we are often unable to isolate such events from the rest of our daily life; instead, we let them completely grip our psyche. Troubling issues at work overflow into our family time.

Dealing with this requires conscious efforts towards living in the present-compartmentalising different aspects of our life and not getting identified with any; realising that thoughts have the habit of amplifying the regrets of the past and fears about the future; becoming open to accepting the reality as it is and not pondering over how it should have been.

Obsessive: This is about our strong need to be perfect. It's an obsession that moulds our outlook at work, with the family, towards diet and exercise, and even in our spiritual pursuits. Accordingly, our mind invariably looks out for what's not going well and that means there's always a sense of lack within.

We need to identify, and attend to, our big priorities in life, rather than trying to be perfect with every single aspect. Further, building a deeper sense of gratitude for all the things that are going well for us supports us in feeling centered.

DIY: Another one is the preference to deal with problems on our own a kind of a 'Do It Yourself approach. When faced with a setback, many of us habitually retreat into a shell to work through our problems. Not seeking help also means brooding over problems longer. Sharing problems with others lightens our load and creates possibilities for new solutions to emerge. This demands a greater willingness to be vulnerable though. Trying it with people you trust offers a suitable starting point.

Set in Stone: The unhappiness gene relates to our conditioned belief that the impact of any negative events would last forever that there's a certain permanency to the unfavourable aspects of our life.

Clearly, this thought process overlooks the reality that nothing is permanent. Favourable and unfavourable events come and go in our life with the regularity of four seasons. Life is a journey of experiences and every setback is indeed a new experience for greater learning and growth. As we create positive beliefs around our setbacks, we feel more empowered and experience greater equanimity.

5

Marriage of Sita

When Sita reaches adulthood, Janaka organizes a *swayamwara* with the condition that Sita would marry only that person who would be able break *Hara Dhanu* (bow of Shiva). Janaka knew, the bow of Shiva was unbreakable for ordinary morals and for selfish person it was not even approachable. Thus, Janaka tries to find the best husband for Sita. When Sita reached adolescence, a *swayamwara* or "self-choice" ceremony was held for the purpose of selecting a suitable husband for her. In order to find the best match for his daughter Sita, King Janaka presented all would-be suitors with the challenge of lifting the bow of Lord Shiva and stringing it. Only the man who performed this heroic task would be able to have Sita's hand in marriage. Rama, prince of Ayodhya, along with his brother Lakshmana and the Sage Vishvamitra were in attendance at this ceremony, and they watched as numerous noblemen failed at stringing the bow. Disappointed, King Janaka poured out his dilemma and misery, sending Lakshmana into a rage at the fact that the monarch had not offered Rama the same test. Upon the invitation of King Janaka, Lord Rama proceeded to lift the bow of Shiva and strung it with ease. So strong and adept was Rama in performing the task that he actually broke the mighty bow in the process of performing the task. With that, not only was Rama's vigor evident to King Janaka, but he had also stolen the heart of Sita, and so the two were wed.

At this time Vishvamitra had brought Rama and Lakshmana to the forest for the protection of sacrifice. Hearing about this *swayamwara*, Vishvamitra asks Rama to participate in the *swayamwara* and takes Rama and Lakshmana to the palace of

Janaka. Janaka is greatly pleased to learn that Rama and Lakshmana are sons of Dasharatha. Next morning, in the middle of the hall, Rama lifts up the bow of Shiva with his left, fastens the string tightly and finally breaks the bow. And thus Rama fulfils Janaka's condition to marry Sita. Later on *Vivaha Panchami*, a marriage ceremony is conducted under the guidance of Satananda. Rama marries Sita, Bharata marries Mandavi, Lakshmana marries Urmila and Shatrughna marries Shrutakirti.

Legend of Shiva's bow is narrated as Vishvamitra asks Janaka to show that bow to Rama and Lakshmana, as they have come this far to have a glimpse of that great bow. Janaka, while narrating its history, makes an offer saying that his daughter Sita will be given in marriage, if only Rama can string the bowstring of Shiva's bow. Here Valmiki informs through Janaka about the nature of birth of Sita, very concisely, which gave raise to too much of debate about this enigmatic Sita and her birth.

Then on performing morning time rites in the aura of next morning, king Janaka invited great soul Vishvamitra, along with *Raghavas*. On reverencing Vishvamitra and the noble souled *Raghavas* according to the formalities envisaged by scriptures, then the virtue souled Janaka spoke these words, indeed.

"Oh, god, you are welcome, oh, holy sage, bid me as to what I should for you, for I am biddable by you, indeed..." So said Janaka.

When said thus by the foreseer Janaka, who can foresee as to why Vishvamitra came with *Raghavas* this far, and thus asked him as to what next is to be done, that sage Vishvamitra, for he is presager and wordsmith, and who knows what is to be done next, said these words in reply to that valiant king Janaka.

"These two are the sons of Dasharatha, well-renowned *Kshatriyas* in world, and they are desirous to see that marvellous bow which has a place with you... You may show that bow, well bodes you, and on beholding that bow the desire of these two princes will come true, and they will go back as they like..."

But Janaka replied the great sage Vishvamitra when he was addressed thus, "I shall firstly tell by which reason that bow has its place here... Oh, godly sage, there was a king renowned as

Devaraata, sixth one from Nimi, the originator of our lineage, and this bow was handed down to him for custodial care by the Sublime Soul, Shiva...

Though much about the Harappan civilisation is a mystery that human remains suggest they were Dravidian. Today, in popular parlance Dravidian connotes a southern an-cestry, with the north being 'Aryan' or of Caucasian descent. In actual fact, however, India is a glorious pot-pouri of races today, so intermingled over several millennia that it is often difficult to separate them geographically anymore.

DNA mapping now offers a realistic assessment of who we are, racially speaking. And the results are often quite surprising which could be why Indians have not taken to it.

Hindus had devised the '*gotra*' system to broadly identify family trees so that marriages were reg-ulated to prevent inbreeding. Of course, the purpose was eventually defeated as families began to stay within caste boundaries for matrimony, no matter how small their numbers, Gene pools were thus bound to shrink.

However, even if a broth of races makes up our genes, the next generation of Indians, at least within certain socio-economic parameters, are adding to it with alacrity. As the inevitable fallout of migration abroad for studies and jobs, many Indians are marrying foreigners of all races, from Caucasian to Mongoloid.

The younger generation born and raised abroad has almost unanimously chosen non-Indians as spouses. Within family we now have people of Scottish, Irish, English, Hispanic, Jamaican, Japanese, German and Polish descent. There's even a Liech tensteiner!

That marks a change from our parents' era when most Indians married within their own ethnicity even though they had settled abroad. Perhaps because, of cultural inhibitions, the farthest they dared to wander to find their mate was perhaps a part of India.

Marrying 'out', of course, had been fairly common in the Indian subcontinent in ancient times. Indigenous people mingled with the innumerable foreign invaders who galloped down the Himalayan passes or landed on our shores from distant lands in search of spices and riches. They often had no other recourse.

The difference in the 21st century is that Indians are the ones venturing abroad and marrying foreigners, instead of the other way round. And it is entirely by choice. As the gene pool undergoes another bout of expansion, the impact on culture, tradition and social norms will be considerable.

Basing on the account that is given by Janaka at the time of Rama's marriage with Sita, Devaraata is the sixth one from Nimi, the originator of Janaka's lineage.

"Once, during the devastation of the Vedic-ritual of Daksha Prajapati, the mettlesome god Rudra, rancorously outstretching the bowstring of this bow, said this to all gods, superciliously...

"'Oh, gods, whereby you have not apportioned my portion of oblations in Vedic-ritual s, as I am also the desirer of such portion, thereby I will shred the highly revered heads of yours with this bow...' So said Shiva to gods."

"Then, oh, best saint Vishvamitra, all gods are truly dismayed, and on their supplicating, *Bhava*, namely Shiva, the God of Gods is gladdened... And that Sublime Soul Shiva gladly gave that bow to all of the great souled gods, and oh, godly saint, then those great souled gods gave this gem of a bow of Shiva, the God of Gods, to our ancestor Devaraata, for custodial care..."

"Later, when I was ploughing the ritual field then raised by the plough from the furrow is a baby girl... since she is gained while consecrating the ritual-field, she is named as Sita, and thus she is renowned..."

"Hers is a non-uterine birth as she surfaced from the surface of the earth, but fostered as my own soul-born girl and I determined to give her in marriage to a bridegroom where his boldness is the only bounty, I receive in that marriage..."

'Dowry is property or money brought by a bride to her husband' and this is familiar throughout the world. In ancient India, there was a counterpart custom to this, called *kanyaa shulkam* meaning 'some bounty, property or money offered by a bridegroom's family to the bride's family' since they are getting a worthy bride, coming into their family, not just as a mere wife of the bridegroom, but to upkeep and promote that family and its progeny. And this dowry or its counterpart is not compulsorily be paid in hard cash, but it may be any kind of gifts mutually exchanged, which has slowly developed into a mega havoc these days. Here Janaka wants the 'valour' of his prospective son-in-law as bounty due to him in the marriage of Sita.

"Oh, eminent sage, as my daughter has surfaced from the surface of earth and has come of age, the kings, having heard my declaration that the bounty for Sita is boldness alone, have come and besought for her... To all of those kings who are beseeching for the girl, I have not given my daughter, saying that she will be given for a bounty of boldness... Then all the kings convoked and on arriving at Mithila, then they wanted to ascertain the calibre of the bow, vis-à-vis their own..."

"For them, those who wanted to ascertain the calibre of the bow, that bow of Shiva is fetched to their proximity, but they are incapable to joggle it, or even to catch hold of it..."

This bow of Shiva will be transported on a wheeled casket-cart with eight wheels and drawn by five thousand robust persons. 'It is drawn by five hundred bulls...' aananda raamayana says so. In other versions of Ramayana, it is said that many people will pull that casket-cart, as one or two persons cannot haul it. Once, when Sita was playing with other girls, their flowery ball of girl's rugby goes under this cart. None of her girlfriends is dare enough to near this bow-casket-cart, since it is a reverential casket-cart. But Sita goes there and pushes that casket-cart aside with her left hand, as though it is a garland, and retrieves that flower ball. This capability of Sita in easy handling of Shiva's bow, becomes a bane to her, when one among the wives of *sapta Rishi* 'Seven Sages...' issues a curse to Sita, saying that 'Sita will be separated from her husband for some time, of course, for the good of people...' So says the tradition.

"Oh, great saint, on knowing the valour of those valorous ones as valueless, I countermanded them... oh, ascetically wealthy Vishvamitra, by that you may know the sequel of it... Then, oh, eminent sage, those kings beleaguered Mithila in a blind fury, since a self-mistrust bechanced among them all, about their own valour..."

"They surmised for themselves that they are brushed off by me, and they possessed by a high rancour, they strangled the City of Mithila..." Then elapsed is an year and in anyway the possessions for livelihood went into a decline, oh, eminent sage, thereby I am highly anguished

"Then I have assuaged the assemblages of gods by my ascesis and gods are also highly gladdened and gave me fourfold forces..."

"Then those evildoers and self-mistrustful kings while being drubbed by the heaven-sent army, they have become vigourless and broken, and they beat a hasty retreat... Oh, tigerly sage this is that supremely radiant bow, and oh, saint of sacred vows, I will show it, even to Rama and Lakshmana..."

"If Rama strings the bowstring of that bow, oh, sage, I will offer my daughter, whose birth is non-uterine, to Dasharatha's Rama..." So said Janaka to Vishvamitra.

Sometime after the wedding, circumstances forced Rama to leave Ayodhya and spend a period of exile in the forests of Dandaka and later Panchavati. Sita willingly renounced the comforts of the palace and joined her husband in braving exile, even living in the Dandaka and Panchavati forests. The Panchavati forest became the scene for her abduction by Ravana, King of Lanka. Ravana kidnapped Sita, disguising himself as a *brahmana* mendicant, or begging holy-man, while her husband was away fetching a magnificent golden deer to please her. Jatayu, the vulture-king, who was a friend of Dasratha (Rama's father), tried to protect Sita but Ravana chopped off his wings. Jatayu survived long enough to inform Rama of what had happened.

Ravana took her back to his kingdom in Lanka, and Sita was held as a prisoner in one of his palaces. During her captivity for a year in Lanka, Ravana expressed his desire for her; however, Sita refused his advances and struggled to maintain her chastity. Hanumana was sent by Rama to seek Sita and eventually succeeded in discovering Sita's whereabouts. Sita gave Hanumana her jewellery and asked him to give it to her husband. However, Hanumana was caught by Lankan forces. Hanumana was about to be executed and burnt in a bonfire when he managed to escape and in return burnt down the Lanka capital city.

Sita was finally rescued by Rama, who waged a famous battle to defeat Ravana. Upon rescue, Rama worried about the future of human society– that any man or women may not use this as an excuse to live with each other without marriage, makes Sita walk on fire to prove her chastity.

Sita in Folk Songs

An ancient Indian folk song depicts a young girl describing to her father the kind of husband she wants. After narrating his various qualities, she say in the end: "Go north, go south, or get for groom from the east, but don't ever go westwards."

Significantly, this song belongs to the region of Mithila, where Sita, heroine of the epic Ramayana was born. More interestingly, Ayodhya, where lived her husband Rama, lies to the west of Mithila. Thus, what this lyric is effectively saying is that a girl from this region would not prefer to have a groom like Rama, which is ironical considering the fact that he is considered the 'perfect man' in the annals of Indian thought. Further, though the numerous temples in this region contain images of both Sita and Rama as a couple, they are invariably named Janaki *Mandirs* (Temples of Sita). Janaki being another epithet for Sita signifying that she is the daughter of king Janaka. Even today, the people of Mithila consider it inauspicious to marry off their daughters in the month of *Marg-Shish*, which is the season when Sita and Rama tied the knot.

These traditions seem less odd when we realize that people all over India, will say approvingly for someone: "He is a Rama like son, a Rama like brother, or a Rama like king. " It is rare however to hear the following as a compliment "Rama like husband or son-in-law."

Intriguing as this phenomena is, the reasons for this all-pervasive sentiment are readily understood when we recall the life adventures of this couple. As is well-known Rama, even though he was its rightful heir, abdicated the royal throne in favor of one of his younger brothers. In addition, he was banished to the forest for fourteen years by his stepmother. Sita, the devoted wife that she was, also accompanied him to his exile. Later, a demon named

Ravana carried her away forcefully and it was only after a fierce war that Rama could regain his virtuous wife. Before accepting her as his queen again however, he asked Sita to publicly prove her chastity, witnessed by all those present in the battlefield.

Thus it is obvious that Sita's trials did not end with her liberation from the demon's captivity. All versions of the Ramayana are unanimous in reiterating her fidelity and devotion towards Rama even in times of extreme adversity. For example, when the hero is preparing to go to exile in the forest all alone, she addresses him thus: "O son of an illustrious monarch, a father, a mother, a brother, a son or a daughter-in-law, all enjoy the fruit of their merits and receive what is their due. It is only the wife who actually shares the fortunes of her husband. When you depart this day for the dense forests which are difficult to penetrate, I shall walk ahead of you crushing under my feet, all the thorns that lie on your way." This is just one of the many expressions Sita used to convince Rama to take her with him. She considered it her privilege to share in his misfortune and suffered the consequent trials and tribulations in equal measure throughout their sojourn in the forest. However, being exiled in the forests was the least of her troubles.

In fact, not even her kidnapping by Ravana could break Sita immense will-power, constantly nourished as it was by the memory of her beloved Rama. Ravana too, fearing the accumulated merits of a chaste woman did not dare touch her; he nevertheless did try' to make advances. What was Sita's reaction to his overtures? The great sage poet Valmiki (author of Ramayana), has captured her wretched condition vividly, through a series of inspired metaphors. For example, on viewing Ravana, "She seemed like a flame wreathed in smoke; a great fame which had dimmed; a lotus pool stripped of its blossoms; like Rohini pursued by Ketu (a metaphor for the eclipsed moon); a traditional text obscured by a dubious interpretation; a faith that has been betrayed; an order that has been flouted; a hope which has been frustrated and an understanding that has grown feeble."

Hanumana Presents Rama's Ring to Sita at *Ashoka-vatika*

Witnessing her appearance, Hanumana, the loyal monkey ally of Rama says: "For a woman the greatest decoration is her lord and Sita, though incomparably beautiful, no longer shines in Rama's absence."

Although her physical beauty undoubtedly dims on account of the enforced separation; she keeps her mind fixed upon Rama, and thus radiates with an inner beauty as a result of this steadfastness. "Though that blessed one was shorn of her own beauty, yet her own soul did not lose its transcendency, upheld as it was by the thought of Rama's glory and safeguarded by her own virtue." Truly she remained chaste in both thought and deed and the various recensions of the epic recall episodes where even the mighty Ravana had to bow before Sita's piety. Once for example, when the demon approached her, she placed a single strand of straw in between them and challenged him to cross the "proverbial last straw." Predictably he did not dare to do so. He knew that the chastity of a virtuous woman was like a fire that could reduce to ashes anyone who tried to violate her against her will.

All of Sita's miseries in the confinement of Ravana pale in comparison however to and humiliation she was subjected to by Rama himself. In a bitter irony, what was deliverance, turned out to be the beginning of another trial.

Abduction of Sita by Ravana

Standing before him, her eyes raised expectantly to his face, the innocent Sita wept, overwhelmed at the prospect of a joyful reunion with her consort after his victory over Ravana. The latter however remained formal and aloof and set out to articulate his heartfelt thoughts (*hrdyaantargatam bhavam*) : "Today I have avenged the insult to my honor and fulfilled my promise. You stand unabashed before me, even though suspicion has arisen with regard to your character. Today you seem extremely disagreeable to me even as a light to one who is suffering from sore eyes. Therefore go wherever you like, O Janaka's daughter, the ten directions are open to you today. What man born in a noble family would take back with an eager mind a woman who has dwelt in another's house, simply because she has been kindly disposed towards him in the past? How can I accept you, who were squeezed into the arms of Ravana while being borne away by him and who regarded you with a lustful eye? There is no more attachment for you in my heart. You may therefore go wherever you like."

Harsh words indeed, which pierced Sita's tender heart like arrows tipped with poison and shrinking within herself, the sensitive lady shed profuse tears, saying: "I was helpless when I came into the contact of Ravana and did not act of my own free will on that occasion. My adverse fate alone is to blame on that score. That which is under my control, viz., my heart, eternally does it abide in you."

The South Indian Ramayana, authored by Kamban, sums up her situation graphically:

Like a deer
on the point of death,
tortured by terrible thirst
in the middle of a desert
who sees a lake
just beyond reach,
she grieved at the barrier
that rose before her.

Addressing her brother-in-law Lakshmana, she says: "Raise for me a pyre, which is the only antidote against this calamity. I no longer desire to survive, smitten as I am with false reproaches." Lakshmana looked at his brother, half-expecting him to put an end to this bewildering public spectacle. Scrutinizing his elder sibling's expression, Lakshmana realized, to his horror, that this was exactly what Rama expected.

Not one of the assembled warriors, who just moments before had proved their mettle in the battlefield, had the courage to dare open his/her mouth opposing the grave injustice being perpetrated. The obedient Lakshmana set out to prepare the pyre. As a mark of respect, Sita circumambulated Rama, who, as the ancient texts put it - stood with his head bent low. As she approached the blazing fires, the world went into a crisis: the immortal gods and living beings, the cosmic elements, the four Vedas and Dharma, all cried out in horror. Then:

As if she were going home
to her place on the lotus
that rises up from the' flooding waters,
she jumped in;
and as she entered, that fire was scorched
by her burning faithfulness.
Goddess Lakshmi

Goddess Lakshmi

The lotus here refers to Sita being an incarnation of the great goddess Lakshmi, who is typically associated with this auspicious flower.

Ravana Fails to Win Over Sita at *Ashoka Vatika*,

Here, to highlight the extremely pure bearing of Sita, the poet has innovatively depicted the moment as being one of an excruciating, fiery torment. Fire is burnt by the heat Sita holds within herself; generated by a lifetime of chastity, self-control, faithfulness, suffering and sacrifice, which are represented here not as abstract ethical virtues but rather as part of the substantial and dynamic reality that suffuses the inner being of a faultless woman like Sita. It was this same heat that had earlier terrified Ravana against coming near her.

Her trial-by-fire is portrayed evocatively in the ancient texts and she not only emerges unsinged, but also manages to scorch the god of fire (*Agni*) himself, who, according to Kamban, screams out in pain and protest. Lifting Sita in his hands, Agni points out that the beads of perspiration formed on her body due to anger directed at her husband were not dried in her hair still continued to bloom as freshly as ever. concentrated energy (*tapas*) proved too much for even the materialize because I could not bear the blazing fire of up by his flames while the flowers she wore Sita's accumulated spiritual force of fire-god, who emerged saying: "I had to faithfulness in this woman."

He also asks Rama:

Didn't you hear
when the gods and sages
and all that moves and is still
in the three worlds
screamed, as they struck their eyes?
Have you abandoned *Dharma*
and resorted to misery instead?

Will rain fall,
will the earth bear its burden
without splitting in two,
will *Dharma* go the right way,
or can this universe survive
if she becomes enraged?
if she utters a curse,
even Brahma on his lotus will die.

Sita's Fire Ordeal

Rama is overjoyed at the developments and the public display of his wife's unblemished character: "Sita undoubtedly needed this purificatory ordeal in the eyes of the people inasmuch as this blessed lady had lived for a long time in Ravana's confinement. The world would have murmured against me saying that my mind was so dominated by lust that I actually accepted the daughter of Janaka without proving her chastity. I too knew Sita to be undivided in her affection to me. Ravana couldn't violate her, protected as she was by her own moral power. In order, however, to convince the inhabitants of the three worlds, I ignored Sita even while she was entering the fire. She is as inseparable from me as sunlight from the sun."

That Sita herself volunteered for the *agni-pariksha* speaks for the high volume of understanding between the couple since she understood Rama's wish without him explicitly stating it. Her action was not a surrender to the unreasonable whims of a husband rather a supreme act of defiance that challenged the aspersions cast on her, by the means of which she highlighted the superficiality of his doubts, so that even the gods had to materialize and point out the apparent fallacy in the indignity he had so unceremoniously cast on her. She emerges as a woman that even *Agni*-who has the power to reduce to ashes everything he touches-dare not touch or harm. Eminent Indian poetess Bina Agarwal has pulled no punches while narrating Sita's dual victimization:

With your husband you chose exile:
suffered privation, abduction,
then the rejection-
the chastity test on scorching flames,
the victim twice victimized.
Could those flames turn to flowers
without searing the soul?
they say you, devoted wife, questioned him not
and let him have his way.

The Desertion of Sita

Thus reconciled, the contended couple repaired back to Ayodhya and Rama continued to rule as an ideal monarch over his extensive rein.

More misfortune however was in store for Sita. No sooner had the couple settled down than rumors started in the capital questioning the propriety of having a queen who had spent a year in a villain's captivity, putting her chastity under doubt. Surprisingly for a clear-headed individual, Rama took these allegations to heart and asked his younger brother Lakshmana to banish Sita (this time alone), to the forests. Rama did this even though he was well aware that his wife was well advanced into the family way.

Thus Lakshmana carried Sita the next morning, on the pretext of visiting the hermitage of a sage, to the forests. The unknowing, innocent lady cheerfully boarded the chariot. Little did she know what travails lay in store for her. Once they reached the wilderness, her brother-in-law informed her thus: "you have been forsaken by the king who is afraid of the ill-report circulating among his citizens. You are to be left near this hermitage by me."

Hearing these cruel words the crestfallen Sita fell swooning to the ground. However, it was not long before the valiant lady composed herself and addressed him thus: "This mortal frame of mine was indeed composed by the creator for bearing sorrow only. What sin was committed by me, that though being of good conduct, I should be forsaken by the king? I cannot give up my life since I carry within myself the seed which will carry forward the lineage of my lord. Do then as you are ordered O son of Sumitra (Lakshmana's mother), forsake me the miserable one, obey the orders of the king, but do tell him this on my behalf: If to preserve your good name among your people, I must be sacrificed, I am content to let it be so. As you serve your subjects, so I serve you."

Rama and Family (Rama, Sita and Lakshmana)

One jarring feature of this whole episode is the role of Lakshmana who is often deified not only as the ideal brother, but also the perfect brother-in-law.

He was known to vent his quick temper whenever he perceived an injustice being perpetrated. In fact when, against the norms of natural justice, Rama was exiled for fourteen years, Lakshmana advised his elder brother to take up arms against their father's decision and seize what was rightfully his by force. Yet when this grave impropriety was being committed on Sita, he was silent, why? In the immortal words of Bina Agarwal:

Your brother-in-law,
so quick to anger
on his brother's behalf, left you,
mother-to-be,
alone in the dark forest,
exiled again.

His brother's command!
some citizen's demand!
was injustice to you
not worthy of his anger?
you, loving sister-in-law,
bore this too is silence
and let him go away.

Thus abandoned, Sita gave birth to twin sons in the wilderness and brought them up all alone, without the protective presence of a father, hence becoming the first single parent in history.

When these worthy sons entered their teens, tales of their valor spread far and wide, and it was not long before Rama realized that they were his own offspring. This knowledge prompted him to immediately call his beloved Sita and the two boys to his court. In front of the assembled subjects, tributary kings, ministers and merchants from all parts of his empire, he asked her to undertake the fire ordeal again for the benefit of these venerable gentlemen, who had missed the earlier spectacle in Lanka.

Sita's reaction however was different from that earlier occasion. The emotional scar had obviously not healed. This time she did not ask her brother-in-law to prepare a funeral pyre for her. Nor did she circumambulate her husband in meek submission. Rather, with folded hands, she merely uttered the following words: "If I have remained true to Rama in mind, speech and action, may the Mother Earth embrace me in her bosom." No sooner had she spoken than the ground beneath her feet split wide open, and before anybody had the time to react, she entered the depths. A dejected and helpless Rama was engulfed in grief. Thus did end the exemplary life of Sita, with fate pursuing her to the bitter end.

In the televised version of the Ramayana, shown in serialized form on Indian television, the Earth Goddess is shown emerging from the ground seated on a bejeweled throne. Spreading out her arms she beckons Sita saying: "Come my child, this world is not worthy of you." Sita does as she is told, leaving behind her, the lamenting assembly.

Sita as Janaki

It is interesting to connect the above episode with the fact that Sita was not only metaphorically (as all woman are), the daughter of the earth, but also literally so, since she had not materialized out of the human womb in the 'normal' manner, rather, she had been found by her father, king Janaka, when he was tilling the fields with a golden plough in fulfillment of a sacred ritual. This is also the reason why the people of Mithila (the place where she was so 'discovered') think of her as the daughter of the whole village because, if Janaka had not ploughed the grounds that day, someone else from the region would have definitely found her and thus she would have become that person's daughter.

Sita's appeal to Mother Earth to reclaim her was not the helpless reaction of slighted woman. It was a spirited, self-effacing statement of protest, when things went beyond endurance. For those of us living in this technologically advanced modern age, Sita's message is extremely significant. As we continue to assail the earth, taking her for granted, she is bound to someday lose patience and cleave open her chest in trepidation, leading to goddess knows what calamity.

Rama's conduct vis-a-vis Sita leaves many questions unanswered. The most significant is of course whether he really doubted her fidelity. Even if we disregard the traditional sentiment believing otherwise, there is a strong logical basis supporting the conventional view:

1) Sometime after he abandoned her, Rama decided to perform the horse sacrifice (*ashvamedha yagya*) which is the highest ritual a king can strive to. There was a technical snag however. Of the hundreds of ceremonies a Hindu has to perform, not one can be performed without a wife. Therefore many in Rama's retinue suggested that he remarry. A suggestion he firmly rejected: "In the heart of Rama there is place for only one woman and that one is Sita." He therefore had a golden image of his wife made and completed the sacrifice. Would anyone thus give his wife a position of such supreme respect if he doubted her chastity?

2) After the vanquish of Ravana, when she was first brought into his presence, Rama compared Sita to a "light," which was hurting his "sore eyes." Thus it is his vision, which finds defect in the bearing of the noble lady, that is at fault, and not the "light" itself, whose natural function is but to illuminate.

3) On the same occasion, before entering the fire, Sita circled Rama clockwise, in respectful homage. What was Rama's reaction during her circulation? Well, he kept his head down (*adhomukham*). Is this not a gesture of self-indictment and contradiction? The ostracized victim is boldly performing what she has set out to do, while her accuser stands with a hung head.

According to Shastri Panduran V. Athavale, a noted social reformer, "It was not Rama who abandoned Sita: in reality it was the king who abandoned his queen. In the effective performance of his duty, he had to choose between a family and the nation. Rama sacrificed his personal happiness for the 'larger' national interest."

In other words, Rama wanted to set a standard, a stainless example for his subjects and followers to look up to. The psychological havoc it may have wreaked on those dependent emotionally on him was of no consequence whatsoever: Thus often does the immediate family of a reformer suffer even though the nation as a collective may gain substantially. Mahatma Gandhi says in his article 'The Law of Suffering,' "Progress is to be measured in terms of the suffering undergone by the sufferer. The purer the suffering, the greater is the progress. Hence did the sacrifice of Jesus suffice to free a sorrowing world. In his onward march he did not count the cost of suffering entailed upon his neighbors, whether it was undergone by them voluntarily or otherwise."

Recall in this context the Mahatma's own neglect of his children, and his imposition of a strict disciplinarian regime on his wife in a drastic manner without preparing her slowly and steadily like he did the entire nation. This is but another instance of the better half being taken for granted, being treated as another experiment in the moral evolution of humanity rather than as a free-minded individual who could have a viewpoint of her own.

Likewise Rama never cared to personally explain anything to his wife; he knew she would understand. These virtuous ladies suffered in silence. What did Kasturba Gandhi as a mother, as a woman, gain out of the high moral pedestal her husband bagged for himself? Her children lacked the presence of a simple, loving father whom they could look up to in an ordinary way. Indeed, it is their 'extraordinariness,' that often distances the path-breaking revolutionaries like Rama and Gandhi from their children who have their own normal, 'selfish aspirations.' In such circumstances a rebellion definitely brews beneath the placid surface. It culminates into the supreme sacrifice of Sita leaving a distraught Rama behind, or it may find expression in objectionable actions (as those of one of the Mahatma's sons), whose sole aim is to bring grief to the 'larger than life' parent. In either case it is the woman of the house who pays the heaviest price. It must be realized here that engrossed in this program of social reform, stress. is placed not only on merely being fair, but equally important is to appear to be 'fair' and 'impartial,' and being theoretically rigid in setting high standards for their own families while being practical and flexible when applying these same principles to the general populace. However, it must go to the credit of both of them they set an equally, if not sterner, moral regime for themselves.

Sita sets a high standard as an ideal wife who stays unswerving in her loyalty and righteousness, no matter how undesirable her husband's response. Her refusal to perform a second *agnipraiksha* and her consequent reversion to mother earth is not merely an act of self-annihilation. It is a momentous and dignified rejection of Rama as a husband. Truly Rama may have deselected her as his queen in deference to social opinion, but it is Sita who rejects him in a personal sense as a husband. By this act does she emerge supremely triumphant. If the defining scale for quantifying greatness is the amount of suffering one has undergone, it is undoubtedly Sita who is the clear winner. It is her dignified tolerance (*sahan-shilta*) and self-effacing silence, which may even be termed as weakness by many, that turns out to be her ultimate emotional strength, far valorous than any assertive aggression. Rightly therefore does her name always precede that of Rama (as in Sita-Ram or Jai Siya-Ram).

In the words of Swami Vivekananda, "There may have been several Ramas, perhaps, but only one Sita."

No other woman has touched the Indian psyche as deeply as Sita has, nor is any other woman enthroned there with as much love as she has been. While feelings for her are uniformly the same in men and women, women naturally identify with her more easily and feel her joys and sorrows, her pains and sufferings, longings and disappointments, far more intensely than men do. To them, whether they are women of the past or present, from among the poorest of the poor or the richest of the rich, from the most advanced communities or from the most backward, educated or uneducated, young or old, her joys and sorrows, pains and sufferings and longings and disappointments are theirs.

While they thus identify with her and relive her life experiences, quite frequently they also transform to her their personal and collective life experiences. Thus we find women giving words to their feelings and emotions, their woes and afflictions, their sense of wretchedness and loneliness and a million other things that are part of every woman's life, in songs, paintings and dances all over the land. Quite often these giving and taking get so mixed up, it is difficult to find out what Sita's feelings are and what the feelings of the woman who sings these songs, paint these paintings and dance these dances are. Perhaps it is not necessary either, because Sita is not a woman who lived several thousand years ago in an India that is dead and gone, but is every woman who was ever born in this land, every woman who ever lived in this land, and every woman who lives here today. Or rather, she is every woman who has ever lived anywhere. Sita is, simply put, everywoman.

One of the most moving, one of the most delicate, beautiful Sita songs is one in which she speaks of her pain as she leaves Ayodhya with Rama to live in the jungle for fourteen years.

In Valmiki's Ramayana, Sita on this occasion appears as a very strong woman: strong in every sense of the word. That the crown of *yuvaraja* has been taken away from her husband does not affect her in the least. In fact, when Rama gives her this news, he is shaking allover, under the force of the fury he has suppressed, his body is covered in perspiration, for such is his disappointment at the crown being snatched away from him. She tells him that going to the jungle and living there has always been her dream, and, in fact, when she was a little girl, astrologers had predicted this. Sita is without any doubt the stronger of the two here when she tells Rama that she shall walk in front of him, crushing the sharp blades of grass and the thorns on his way with her feet and thus making his path smooth for him; when she says that she shall expect nothing from him while they are in the jungle, not even conjugal pleasures - for she assures him she is going to live in the jungle as a *brahmacharani*, giving up all pleasure of the flesh. No amount of persuasion from Rama asking her to stay back in Ayodhya can persuade her. She tells him she knows where her place is, when he goes to the jungle it is with him in the jungle, and nothing in the world can stop her from going with him. The fears of the jungle, the inconveniences that Rama so eloquently paints before her do not affect her in the least. And when Rama still refuses to allow her to go with him in spite of all she says, she questions his masculinity itself, thus forcing him to take her with him. It is indeed a very strong Sita that we see here.

Yet deep inside, we never miss the feeling that behind all this show of bold strength, there is a woman who is tenderness itself, who is vulnerability itself. We feel that along with this diamond-like Sita that we see, there is also a lotus-like Sita, tender and delicate, whom a passing wind can destroy.

In fact, we do not have to wait long to see her. We see this Sita in her helplessness and confusion at the time of the leave taking, which Valmiki paints with superb poetic skill.

Unable to change Kaikeyi's mind, a frustrated and furious Dasharatha announces that he will send all his wealth, all the grains stored, his army, his priests, all with Rama to the jungle. Kaikeyi objects to this. When further attempts to change her mind fails, Dasharatha, tired and wailing now, announces that he will follow Rama to the jungle, and all the people of Ayodhya too will go with them, leaving the kingdom for Kaikeyi and Bharata to enjoy alone. It is then that Rama announces this will not do, he has already given up all the royal comforts, he has decided to live on the simple fruits and roots of the jungle, like ascetics, and therefore he has no need for the army and other things Dasharatha has been talking about. He then asks for valkalas, cloths of grass or bark that ascetics wear, to be brought in so that he can wear them to the jungle. Kaikeyi herself goes and brings a bunch of these and Rama picks up and wears a set, followed by Lakshmana. Sita looks at the cloths still left for her wearing and gets a fright, 'as a deer at the sight of the snare.' She takes two pieces of cloths made of *kusha* grass and then becomes completely embarrassed, for she does not know how to put them on. With her eyes full of tears, she asks Rama how the ascetics wear them. In her mortification, her mind ceases to work properly, she does not know what do, and she gets vexed repeatedly. Thoroughly perplexed now, she puts one piece of the *valkala* around her neck and waits with the other in her hand.

If the strong woman who fights boldly for her right to be with as he goes to jungle is Sita, this helpless, vulnerable woman unaware of all life other than the royal life she has been used to from her birth, the woman who gets easily mortified in embarrassment and whose eyes readily fill with tears, too is Sita.

It is this Sita that awakens the fury of a sage like Vasishtha, fills his eyes with tears and makes him shout at Kaikeyi for her cruelty and tell her that Sita would not go to the jungle, but would, instead, sit on the throne in place of Rama and rule Ayodhya.

And it is this Sita that makes every woman in the palace of Ayodhya weep for her in uncontrollable anguish as she prepares to leave for the jungle with Rama.

A tender, beautiful scene takes place in the midst of all chaos, as Sita gets ready to leave for the jungle. Kausalya comes forward and gathers her in her arms and holds her tightly to herself.

For this wonderful woman of unsurpassed beauty, strong and vulnerable at the same time, adored by all, has an equally wonderful place in the heart of her mother-in-law too.

In the Indian culture, as in most other cultures, a woman leaves her home and her people and goes and becomes a member of her new family when she gets married. Because she comes from another home, has often been used to a different way of living, and because she comes to take the central place in her man's heart, there are frequently rivalries between her and her mother-in-law. Classical literary works as well as folktales and songs are full of such rivalries.

However, in the Ramayana, we see this rivalry totally absent between Sita and her mother-in-law Kausalya. The folksong also sings of the beautiful relation between these two women, one worshipped wherever Indian culture has reached as the mother of the God-incarnate and the other as his wife.

On her way to the jungle, Sita speaks again and again of how she misses her mother-in-law. She is tired and asks Rama to go slow. What has drained her of energy, exhausted her, is not the walk really, for it is not about the distance they have covered she talks about, nor is it about the difficulties on the path. There is no talk about the heights she had to climb, nor about thorns on the way, or stones, or other difficulties. What has really tired her is what she has left behind. And of all that she has left behind, what she misses more than anything else is the love of Kausalya. For, she says she misses the nose ring she has left behind in Ayodhya, she misses her *hasuli*, the neck ornament she has left behind, she misses her anklet, she misses her thin sari, she misses Ayodhya itself, but each thing she misses reminds her how she misses Kausalya, of whom she speaks again and again.

In a land where women dread their mothers-in-law more than anything else in the world, and perhaps rightly too, this Sita song is a tribute to a mother-in-law who lavished her love on her daughter-in--law.

The song is also eloquent about another side of Sita about which Valmiki does not tell us much: Sita as a young woman brought up in comforts, with such a young woman's, or perhaps every woman's, love for the fine things of life, particularly for fine clothes and ornaments. A nose ring, an anklet, a *hasuli*, a fine sari... True, the love for these things that women show often puzzles men, but the love for such things too is perhaps part of being a woman, and is found universally in women, whether it is a result of cultural conditioning or her natural inheritance. The song also tells us that the powerful Sita, who in spite of her total and complete love for Rama, defies him and leaves him behind to enter the earth and disappear from his life forever, unwilling to accept injustice and humiliation at his hands, is also an ordinary woman, with all her strengths and weaknesses.

6

Sufferings of Sita

Sita's sufferings as also the slaying of Vali as depicted in our Puranic literature has agitated the minds of many Rama *Bhaktas*. Late Sri C. Rajagopalachari (Rajaji) in his Ramayana and Shri Narayana Bhattathiri in his Narayaneeyam have dealt with this subject and stated their views. Their comments are reproduced below; these may also be seen reproduced in the web-site:

> "if we keep in mind that when God takes a lower and limited form by His own ordinance, limitations follow and we should not be confused thereby. This is my humble view as against other explanations propounded by the pious."
>
> "Valmiki has it that Rama gave some explanation with which Vaali was satisfied. But I am omitting all this as pointless and pray that the learned may forgive me. What I think is that an *avataar* is an *avataar* and that among the sorrows that the Lord and His consort had to endure in their earthly incarnation, this liability to have their actions weighed on the earthly scale is a part."

Rama's face showed a strange transformation of mind. None of those around him, not even Lakshmana, could understand.

> "I have slain the enemy," said Rama (to Sita). "I have recovered you. I have done my duty as a Kshatriya. My vow is now fulfilled." ......"It was not for mere attachment to you that I waged this grim battle; but it was in the discharge of duty as a Kshatriya. It gives me no joy now to get you back, for dubiety envelopes you like a dark cloud of smoke."

"What do you wish to do now?" he continued. "You must live alone, for we cannot live together. You can stay under the protection of any of our kinsmen or friends. How can a Kshatriya take back a wife who has lived for so long in a stranger's house?"

Sita looked at Rama. Her eyes flashed fire. "Unworthy words have you spoken!" she said. "My ears have heard them and my heart is broken. The uncultured may speak such words, but not one nobly born and brought up like you......................Is it my fault that the wicked *Raakshasa* seized me by force and imprisoned me? But since this is how you look at it, there is but one course open to me."

Then, turning to Lakshmana, she said:

"Fetch the faggots, Lakshmana, and kindle a fire."

Obeying Sita, Lakshmana kindled a big fire and the princess, with eyes fixed on the ground, circumambulated her Lord and exclaimed: "Ye Gods, I bow before you. Oh *Rishis*, I bow to you. Oh Agni, you at lease know my purity and will take me as your own!"

With these words she jumped into the flames. And wonder of wonders! The lambent flames were crowded with celestial figures; for all the gods came and assembled there.

Brahma spoke: "Narayana! Mighty God that took human form to slay Ravana! Is not this your own Lakshmi?"

Agni, God of fire rose in his own body out of the flames and lifting Sita in his arms with all her clothes and jewels untouched and intact, presented her to Rama.

Rama said to Brahma:

> "Who am I? All that I know and can tell is that I am Rama, son of Dasaratha. You must know who I am and whence I came and more; it is you who must inform me."

Rama accepted Sita fire-proved saying to her: "Think you that I did not know your irreproachable purity? This ordeal was to satisfy the people................" So saying, he drew her to his side.

Then Dasaratha descended from above and, placing the prince on his lap, blessed him.

> "My child!" he said to Sita. "Forgive my son. Forgive him for the wrong he did to you to preserve the dharma of the world. God bless you."

I have followed the story of the Prince of Ayodhya as told by Valmiki. There was a legend current among people, I think even before Valmiki's time, that after recovering Sita, for fear of scandal, Rama sent her away to live in the forest. This pathetic episode must have sprung from the sorrow-laden imagination of our women. It has taken shape as *Uttarakaanda* of Ramayana.

Although there is beauty in the *Uttarakaanda* I must say my heart rebels against it. Valmiki had disposed of this old legend through the fire ordeal in the battle field. Even that ordeal does not seem to me as consistent with Rama's character. It is painful to read it.

As the Prince returned from Mithila he met Parasurama. I have heard it said that with that meeting, Parasurama's *Avataar* came to an end. Likewise, it should be held, I think, that Rama's *avataar* came to an end with the slaying of Ravana. After that battle, Rama remained only as a king of the Ikshvaku race. On this theory, Rama's treatment of Sita after the battle and in the *Uttarakaanda* can be explained simply as the behaviour of a king in accordance with the customs of the time.

Narayana Bhattatiri's comments in his Narayaneeyam:

In Canto 35 Verse 10 of Narayaneeyam, Narayana Bhattatiri attempts to explain Rama's action after slaying Ravana, resulting in Sita Devi's ordeal by fire and again, later in Ayodhya, when he sent her away to the forest even though she was pregnant.

The following translation is from Narayaneeyam published by Sri Ramakrishna Math, Madras (March 1976):

> "This human embodiment of Thine is for instructing mankind how too much attachment (*Kama*) will lead to pangs of separation and how addiction to *Dharma* (the letter of the Law) will push one to such *Adharma* as abandonment of innocent ones. Otherwise, it is unimaginable how Thou,

who art ever established in the *Atman*-consciousness, canst ever have any weakness of the mind. O Thou Lord of Guruvayoor, the very embodiment of *Sattwa*, deign to remove my sufferings from this disease."

The following comment appears in Note appended to the text:

"Bhattar's estimate of Rama Incarnation, that it is to show men how intense affection (*Kama*) will lead us to pangs of separation (as Rama suffered from his loss of Sita) and how extreme addiction to *Dharma*, (the letter of the Law), will push one to *Adharma*–is an echo of the Bhagawata verse 5.19.5-6. Many a devotee of Rama will not agree with this, although it may be conveying a subtle point that would interest a critical student. Rama and Krishna are two major incarnations, the former being glorified in the Ramayana and the latter in the Bhagawata."

Both have been equally important factors in the devotional life of India. Rama Incarnation depicts a model of manhood and human conduct which people are asked to follow, whereas Krishna is a Divine manifestation whose words are to be followed but not deeds. In some Vaishnava texts, Rama is therefore described as *Maryada-Purushottama* (Divinity who has restricted Himself by laws) and Krishna as *Pushti-Purushottama* (Divinity that bestows Grace in ways that are not bound by laws and social norms.)

Slaying of Vaali-Rajaji's Account

"All who are born must die. This is the law. I do not therefore grieve for my death. Still, your sin is great in killing me in this treacherous way." This, Vaali, son of Indra, reproached Rama with his dying breath. And all this is fully set out by Valmiki, the divine poet, as well as by Kamban. Against this accusation what defence could Rama offer?

Valmiki has it that Rama gave some explanation with which Vaali was satisfied. But I am omitting all this as pointless and pray that the learned may forgive me. What I think is that an *avataar* is an *avataar* and that among the sorrows that the Lord and His consort had to endure in their earthly incarnation, this liability to have their actions weighed on the earthly scale is a part.

Rama erred in running after the magic deer to please his wife. Consequent to this, difficulties and sorrows and conflicts of duty pursued him. If we keep in mind that when God takes a lower and limited form by His own ordinance, limitations follow and we should not be confused thereby. This my humble view as against other explanations propounded by the pious."

Sita was a foundling, discovered in a furrow in a ploughed field, and for that reason is regarded as a daughter of Bhudevi, the Goddess Mother Earth. She was found and adopted by Janaka, hence she was also called Janaki, king of Mithila in present day Nepal and his wife Sunayana. Since she was the princess of Mithila, she was (and is also) known as Maithili. Upon her coming of age, a *swayamwara* was held to select a suitable husband for her, and she was wed to Rama, prince of Ayodhya, an *avataar* of Vishnu. Sita is the consort of Lord Rama, the seventh *avataar* (incarnation) of Lord Vishnu. Sita is the one of the most popular goddesses of Hindu religion.

Devi Sita is regarded as the incarnation of Goddess Lakshmi, the divine consort of Lord Vishnu. Sita is considered as the ideal daughter, ideal wife, and ideal mother, since ages. Goddess Sita is remembered for her virtues and attributes. Devi Sita symbolizes all that is noble in womanhood.

Sita is one of the principal characters in The Ramayana. Her entire life constitutes an example of idealism. Sita is a perfect example of loyalty and morality. Goddess Sita leaves the palace charms and amenities, in order to stay in exile with her husband. During the period of exile, Sita was abducted by the demon-king Ravana and imprisoned for months, in Lanka. When Sita got freed from the clutches of Ravana, she proved her sanctity to Lord Rama by giving *Agni-Pariksha* (Fire Ordeal). Sita is regarded as the role model of wifely love and adherence to duty. Sita is a brave woman of extraordinary brilliance. She has got all the values that people believe, a woman must have in her character. Sita is a woman of virtue and of immeasurable patience. Through her great character, she has captured hearts of millions of people.

The events and places related to the life of Shri Rama and Sita are true cultural and social heritage of every Indian irrespective of caste and creed.

Sita's life was interpreted and sought to be emulated in today's context. However, there is no escaping the fact that in north India the Sita of popular imagination has been deeply influenced by the Sita of Ramcharit Manas by Tulsi. In most other versions of the Ramayana, close companionship and joyful togetherness of the couple are the most prominent features of the Rama-Sita relationship rather than her self-effacing devotion and loyalty which have become the hallmark of the modern day stereotype of Sita. The medieval Ramayana of Tulsi marks the transition from Rama and Sita being presented as an ideal couple to projecting each of them as an ideal man and woman respectively. *Agni Pariksha* translates as "trial by fire." Ravana abducted Sita and held her captive for several months in his kingdom of Lanka. This forced Rama to invade Lanka, kill Ravana and free his wife. But before accepting her he asked her to give the *Agni Pariksha.* She had to immerse herself in burning flames and come out unscathed in order to prove that she was unsullied. This has created a controversy and given ammunition to Hindu baiters.

The Moral Dilemma of the *Agni Pariksha*

In the 21st century if a woman is abducted, as Sita was, it would be considered heinous and unacceptable for her husband to demand a trial by fire. At least this would be the case in societies that believe in the equality of the genders. And by this benchmark Rama grievously erred in asking Sita to undergo the *Agni Pariksha*. But this event did not take place in the 21st century. It took place 7,000 years ago. Even 700 years ago women in all parts of the world were subject to exploitation. Hence the morality of events of ages gone by must be judged by the standards of those ages and not by current sensitivities. In the Valmiki Ramayana Rama forgets that he is God, when he disowns Sita and compels her to enter the burning pyre. To the assembled deities he says, "I think of myself to be a human being, by name Rama, the son of Dasharath." The deities then remind him that he is the *avataar* of the Supreme God. When Sita emerges from the flames Rama says that though he knew that Sita was pure the *Agni Pariksha* was essential to prove her fidelity before the society at large. Despite the rationalization attempted the morality of the act can still be questioned. One cannot compel someone to undergo torture in the guise of exoneration by society. Tulsidasa in his Ramcharita Manas adds an interesting twist. Before Sita is abducted Rama tells her that he will have to engage in some *lila* or play acting in which she would be abducted and made to suffer. He asked her to take refuge with Agni, the demi-God of Fire, and leave behind her image so that the image would face the tribulations and not the real Sita.

During the *Agni Pariksha* Agni consumes the image and returns the real Sita to Rama. None of those witnessing the trial by fire can make this out. They think that Sita is proving her fidelity. This may seem another form of rationalization, but the simplicity of the idea and lyrical poetry used to describe it has to be lauded. "The image and the social taint both perished in the fearsome flames. The deities and sages watching were unable to fathom what really happened. Agni led the real Sita, the one worshipped by all, from the flames. And returned her to Rama......."

Rama may have forsaken Sita, but the power of popular sentiment has kept them united. Her name precedes Ram's in the popular greeting in North India: Jai Siya Ram, as also in several *bhajans* and chants. He is seen as incomplete without her.

His rejection of Sita is almost universally condemned while her rejection of him is held up as an example of supreme dignity. By that act she emerges triumphant and supreme, she leaves a permanent stigma on Rama's name. I have never heard even one person, man or woman, suggest that Sita should have gone through the second fire ordeal quietly and obediently and accepted life with her husband once again, though I often hear people say that Ram had no business to reject her in the first place.

Disqualified Husband

The rejection of Rama by Sita has come to acquire a much larger meaning in popular imagination than one woman's individual protest against the injustice done to her. It is a whole culture's rejection of Rama as a husband. For instance, people will say approvingly: "He is a Rama-like son, a Rama-like brother, or a Rama-like king." But they will never say as a mark of approval, "He is a Rama-like husband." If Rama had not been smart enough to win Sita for a wife by his skill in stringing Shiva's bow, if instead Janaka had decided to match their horoscope and it had predicted that Sita would be abandoned by him, I doubt that Ram would have ever found a wife. No father would have consented to give his daughter to a man like Rama - his claims to godlike perfection notwithstanding. Most people I talked to echoed this sentiment: "*Rama honge bade admi par Sita ne kya sukh paya*?" (Ram may have been a great man, but what good did it do Sita?)

Agni Pariksha

As could be expected, Sita was overjoyed at the thought of embracing Rama once again after he had rescued her. Rama, however, refused to look at her, excoriating her on the basis of the fact she has lived in the house of another man. Rama informed Sita that he had fought the war solely for the purpose of avenging the dishonor that Ravana had done him, and that she was now free to go with whatever man she wished. This sudden turn of events left all onlookers shocked and mystified. Sita was understandably devastated by Rama's actions, and, shaking with grief and humiliation, begged Lakshmana to build her a pyre upon which she could burn herself alive, as the thought of life without Rama filled her with insurmountable despair. At this point, Lakshmana grew angered with Rama for the first time in his life, but, following his brother's order, he built a pyre for Sita nonetheless. While the onlookers stood paralyzed with the sheer pathos of the display, Sita walked slowly into the fire. But to their even greater shock and amazement, she was miraculously unharmed by the flames, instead glowing radiantly from where she stood at the center of the pyre. Rama interpreted this as confirmation of her purity, since Agni, the fire god, would surely have destroyed the impure and sinful, and he immediately ran to Sita to embrace her. He had never doubted her purity for a second, but, as he would later explain to Sita, the people of the world would not have accepted or honored her as a queen or a woman if she had not passed this test, commonly referred to as the *Agni pariksha.*

The Thailand version of the Ramayana, however, tells of Sita walking on the fire, of her own accord, to feel clean, as opposed to jumping in it. She is not burnt, the coals turn to lotuses. Walking on live coals is still a common custom in the south of India.

Abandonment and Later Life

The couple came back to Ayodhya, where Rama was crowned king with Sita by his side. While Rama's trust and affection for Sita never wavered, it soon became evident that some people in Ayodhya could not accept Sita's long captivity under the power of Ravana.

Upon returning to Ayodhya, Rama was crowned King and Sita was to be his queen. However, in spite of her survival of the *Agni pariksha*, it soon became evident that a significant percentage of the citizenry of Ayodhya still doubted her chastity, considering the persuasive power of Ravana and the sheer length of time she had been held captive by him. Hence, these unconvinced citizens were of the opinion that Sita was unfit to be queen. Although Rama knew in his heart that these aspersions cast on Sita were entirely baseless, he nevertheless felt that his responsibilities to his citizens as a ruler superseded his responsibilities to his wife as a husband. This one-pointed sense of duty led Rama to order the banishment of Sita from his household, and, ever the faithful wife, Sita complied with his command.

Thus, once again Sita was in exile, but this time all by herself and also pregnant, at that. She sought refuge in the hermitage of the sage Valmiki, where she delivered twin sons, Lava and Kusha. Sita raised her sons single-handedly in the hermitage, and they grew to be valiant and intelligent. Eventually they were united with Rama, and, upon witnessing this acceptance of her children by their father, Sita sought final refuge in the arms of her original mother Bhumidevi. Hearing her plea for release from an unjust world and from a life that had rarely been happy, the earth dramatically split open and Bhudevi manifested herself, taking Sita away. Although Rama demanded Sita's return, the earth remained closed, and Rama lived out the remainder of his life in sorrow, never remarrying. Instead, he ordered the construction of a golden idol of Sita which he used from that point on at rituals requiring the presence of a wife.

During Rama's period of rule, an intemperate washer man, while berating his wayward wife, declared that he was "no pusillanimous Rama who would take his wife back after she had lived in the house of another man." This statement was reported back to Rama, who knew that the accusation of Sita was baseless. Nevertheless, he would not let slander undermine his rule, so he drove Sita out.

Sita was thus forced into exile a second time; she was not only alone this time but also pregnant. Abandoned Sita wandered about in the forest and at last reached the hermitage of Valmiki who gave her refuge in his hermitage, where she delivered twin sons named Kusha and Lava. The other hermits did not like and discouraged Valmiki for giving Sita shelter and protection and they said "Sita is impure, otherwise her husband would not have abandoned here."

In the hermitage, Sita raised her sons alone, as a single mother. They grew up to be valiant and intelligent, and were eventually united with their father. Once she had witnessed the acceptance of her children by Rama, Sita sought final refuge in the arms of her mother (Bhûmi). Hearing her plea for release from an unjust world and from a life that had rarely been happy, the earth dramatically split open; Bhûmi appeared and took Sita away to a better world.

While the Ramayana mostly concentrates on Rama's actions, Sita also speaks many times during the exile. The first time is in the town of Chitrakuta where she narrates an ancient story to Rama, whereby Rama promises to Sita that he will never kill anybody without provocation.

The second time Sita is shown talking prominently is when she speaks to Ravana. Ravana has come to her in the form of a Brahminand Sita tells him that he doesn't look like one.

Some of her most prominent speeches are with Hanumana when he reaches Lanka. Hanumana wants an immediate union of Rama and Sita, and thus he proposes to Sita to ride on his back. Sita refuses as she does not want to run away like a thief; instead she wants her husband Rama to come and defeat Ravana to save her.

A female deity of agricultural fertility by the name Sita was known before Valmiki's Ramayana, but was overshadowed by more well-known goddesses associated with fertility. According to the Ramayana, Sita was discovered in a furrow when Janaka was ploughing. Since Janaka was a king, it is likely that plowing was part of a royal ritual to ensure fertility of the land. Sita is considered to be the child of the Mother Earth, produced by the union between the king and the land. Sita is a personification of the Earth's fertility, abundance, and well-being.

Sita has been a much revered figure amongst the Hindus. In the blurring of the boundary between religion and mythology, between history and fiction, she has been portrayed as an ideal daughter, an ideal wife, and an ideal mother. These portrayals of her never change, and are more or less constant in various texts, stories, illustrations, and even movies and modern media. Sita is often worshipped with Rama as his consort. The occasion of her marriage to Rama is celebrated as *Vivaha Panchami.*

The actions, reactions and instincts manifested by Sita at every juncture in a long and arduous life are deemed exemplary; Her story has been portrayed in the book *Sitayanam*. The values that She enshrined and adhered to at every point in the course of a demanding life are the values of womanly virtue held sacred by countless generations of Indians.

What is ambiguous is her portrayal as an ideal queen. Was she a good states person? Was she a warrior? Her sacrifices and actions are most often portrayed in her personal capacity and not as a governance figure. Sita was abducted because she had to step out of the safety line to give alms to Ravana disguised as a Brahmin. The giving of alms to Brahmin in those times was more of a duty to be performed, rather than an optional charitable act. This held true more so for the royals and they were to lead by example. Also, the incident of Sita's refusal to come back with Hanumana like a common thief, her renunciation of queen-hood and exile from Ayodhya after her return. All her key aspects are shown in a favourable light, but not as a head of state, but as an ideal woman. This is in stark contrast to Rama, who is always portrayed also as an ideal king who was just and fair and always thought of his people before all else in addition to being depicted as an ideal husband and an ideal son.

Popular culture sees Sita as an *abla nari* or a helpless woman. She is portrayed as someone who needs support and assistance of the male folk in the myth. However, this would have to be balanced with Sita's steadfast demonstration of honor and dignity, compelling her to both enter the fire and to ask Mother Earth to take her from a setting filled with pain and misunderstanding. In this light, Sita becomes a complex figure of what it means to be a woman.

Depiction

As a traditional archetype (though frequently criticized in modern times) of feminine beauty and grace in the Hindu religion, Sita is often depicted in Indian art, sculpture and iconography as a resplendent woman with pleasant facial features. She is fair-skinned with long, black hair, though her head is sometimes covered by an elaborate head-dress in order to communicate her queenly status. As could be expected of her social status, she is often bejeweled with bracelets and anklets of gold. She wears a *sari*, which symbolizes her chaste and virtuous nature. Her physiognomy is almost always anthropomorphic, though she may be depicted with additional arms in images attempting to speak to her status as an incarnation of Lakshmi. In religious iconography, she is usually seated or standing at the left side of her husband Rama, as well as any number of other important characters from the Ramayana including Hanumana, Lakshmana, her twin sons, and sometimes even Ravana. Such pictures often depict famous scenes from the Hindu epic.

Worship

With the composition of Tulsidas' devotional *Ramcarit manas* came the increasing popularity of Rama in popular worship. With this came increased theological significance for Sita, as well. Together, Rama and Sita came to be conceived of as the supreme divine couple, male and female aspects of god, and were invoked as such in religious practice. In contemporary Hinduism, Sita is identified as a goddess and is a common focus of worship, however, she has not attained the status of a powerful, independent deity in and of herself. Accordingly, it is rare to find a temple dedicated to Sita alone. Instead, her idol is most often found in temples dedicated to Rama or Hanumana, installed alongside her husband and other important characters from the Ramayana. She is approached by worshipers not as deity who provides blessings, but rather as an intermediary figure who can petition her husband for the dispensation of grace upon human beings. In spite of this trend, some Sakta groups, particularly those in eastern India, have identified Sita as the dominant member of her relationship with Rama.

Sita is a central character in a number of popular Hindu festivals. *Vivah Panchmi* in Hindi *Aghan* Month, is considered the wedding anniversary of Rama and Sita. On this day, worshippers perform marriage celebrations for small statues of Sita and Rama in their houses. In the evening, these statues are taken onto the streets in a grand procession. For the duration of *Vivah Panchmi*, temples are festooned with elaborate decorations, and readings of the Ramayana take place. All the while, Hindus worldwide direct their prayers to Rama and Sita, as well as their close companions. Sita is also widely acknowledged alongside her husband during the ten day *Vijayadashami* festival, appearing as a major character in a dramatic performance of the Ramayana called the *Rama-lila*, which is performed throughout India. Furthermore, during *Diwali* (the Festival of Lights) in North India, lamps and candles are customarily lit in order to reenact the legend that oil lamps were lit along the path to Ayodhya to guide Rama and Sita back home after Ravana had been defeated.

Controversy

Traditionally, Hinduism has championed Sita as the role-model and epitome of domestic wifely duty towards one's husband. Her elevated status in Hindu mythology, however, has recently been tarnished and criticized by Indian feminists who see Sita as an overly-submissive wife who committed suicide for an ultimately untrusting husband. Sita's ideal qualities are presented in the Ramayana to be her unquestioned subordination to the demands of her husband. Many Indian feminists therefore reject Sita as the archetype of women's rights. In their reassessments of the Ramayana, they have concluded that Sita's behavior is not worthy of emulation and instead identify Draupadi as a better role model based upon her confidence and resolve.

Another controversial element surrounding Sita's mythology is her test by fire *(Agni pariksha)* and her later abandonment by Rama altogether in the *Uttarakanda*, the last book of the epic. Due to these disturbing developments in the narrative, some later poets such as Kampan, author of the *Tamil Ramayana*, and Vishvanatha Satyanarayana, author of the *Telugu* version, have left out the latter part of the book entirely. In congruence with these developments in the narrative, modern Indological scholarship has suggested that the *Uttarakanda* section of the Ramayana was interpolated into the story later than books two through six, thus emancipating the "true" Rama of responsibility for his mistreatment of Sita. Accordingly, many Hindus today accept a version of the Ramayana in which Sita and Rama live together happily after Rama is crowned king.

As a feminist Issue

From a feminist perspective, Sita's story is illustrative of subjugation of women in Hindu culture especially in comparison to Durga who is a symbol of female raw force:

- She fits the classic damsel in distress stereotype, waiting to be rescued by a man. Indeed she takes it a step further and refuses to be rescued by anyone other than *her* man.
- She alone is suspected of adultery by Rama and her subjects, and forced to prove her innocence. Rama is never asked to undergo the trial by fire to prove he was faithful to her, and neither is he doubted by his subjects or by Sita.
- Rama banishes Sita to the forest for merely having been accused of adultery by citizens of Ayodhya.
- Years later, when Rama meets her again through coincidence, he hesitates to take her back, causing Sita to call up her mother Bhûmi and be subsumed into the earth (which may arguably be a metaphor for suicide).

Thus from a feminist perspective, to hold Sita up as an example of the ideal woman and wife is to endorse male supremacy and female subservience; and to endorse Rama as the ideal husband is to endorse misogyny. There is evidence that this "Sita Syndrome" encourages domestic violence and subjugation of women in the subcontinent and Diaspora communities.

Birth of Sita *Mata*-Example of Women Hood and Women suffering in Today's society?

There are many aspects to look at when we appreciate this worldly mother, the philosophical aspect, the spiritual aspect and then the physical aspect in which the worldly people (i.e. common man) identifies with.

Philosophical Aspect

How do we look at Sita *Mata* in a Philosophical manner? What does she represent, what is her ideals in respect to children, husband and family? She represents a perfect woman, a mother, sister and daughter. She is the divine *param shakti* that resides all over, that *param shakti* existed at all times, it has no starting or ending-this could be hard to fathom, but every source has an energy point, the dawn of everything is that divine spark, the *param shakti*. Sita *Mata* is the worldly mother that seeks the best interest for us all, she is the name we call in our time of need, in our time of hunger and thirst. She represents the values and culture of women, she represents the challenges women face in society through all ages.

Spiritual Aspect

The Divine Devi represents a mother that can ease our troubled minds, raise our spirituality and love. In the Ramayana, Sita represents our love, the pure bliss that can be attained by surrendering to the feet of God. When Ravana (represents uncontrolled senses, evil tendencies and the *Rajasic* quality) captures Sita *Mata* (our inner love/bliss), looking and praying to that divine power (Shri Sita Ram-Yes Sita as well, as Half of Sita is Ram and half of Ram is Sita etc), thus Shri Rama slays (tames our senses, destroys evil and the *Rajasic* qualities) Ravana and freeing Sita *Mata* (our inner divine bliss). Shri Sita *Mata* is inside all of us, we have been captured by Ravana in some moments in life (i.e. arguing, hatred or anger) we tend to lock away that inner beauty, that divine love inside of us (Sita *Mata*). We must use the key of the Lord's grace to unlock our true selves, show the world that we are divine and loving just like Sita *Mata* and we will bring out the Sita *Mata* in everyone. Ask that divine Shakti, O Lord, control my thoughts so they may be positive and helpful to all. The Divine Sita *Mata* guides us all, the divine love inside of us truly guides us all.

Physical Aspect

Many questions arise when we look at the Divine Mother and her path in life from youth to the time of marriage then as she goes into the forest with Shri Rama. Many events take place, but some of the challenging and sad point that many see as societies downfall is when she went through *Agnipravesham.*

Before we act or think with anger or impluse, we must always remember, Lord Vishnu's *Lilas* are *Achinthya* and *Adbhutha*. Which simply means beyond the Comprehension of common man. At times you need to think impassionately to understand these Intricacies [*But do not lose the lesson/reason and why she suffered and the pains she went through due to society's view of Women. More on this below*]. Do not get caught up in the suffering or physical pains, these are done to show many aspects of life as human beings on earth with the divine spark inside of us. We must look at Sita *Mata* as a representation of Women around the world, the divine *devi* that sustains life is that supreme *Shakti*. We as society should understand how we treat women and value them in a greater light. The suffering by Sita *Mata* on a physical level was to also show the world of the pressures and challenges women face in this day and age. In a man dominated world, Sita *Mata* shows the struggles that women face in every age. We must always treat women, especially those that are close to us in our lives as Goddesses on earth, they hold special powers that men cannot comprehend. I always believe God will listen to a mother before a father, reason being is that a mother has a spiritual connection that goes beyond realms when it comes to a child. Sita *Mata*'s pains and suffering must never be taken for granted, although it was on a *Achinthya* and *Adbhutha* level, we must derive the lessons and learn from them.

To add to the physical sadness that was imposed on Sita, let us look at another event; the abonishment of Sita by Balakrishnan M; "Regarding Sita's banishment, in *Uttara Kanda*, Lord Ramachandra demonstrated, the ideal king should look at the interest of the country that his own personal interest. Remember that Lord Rama, belong to line of Ishvaku, Harichandra, Aja and etc where the kings even willing to sacrifice their own life to uphold dharma. Even Lord Rama once said to Sita in *Aranya kandam* that he was willing to give up Lakshamana, Sita and his own life to uphold dharma. It was the conflict between the duty of the king and duty as the husband. Well, what would you do if you were caught in that position?"

It was not an easy decision to make. Even in modern days, in management of organization a classical management writer by the name of Henri Fayol in one of his 14 principles of management said the individual interest must be subordinate to organizational interest. So in Bhagavad Gita Chapter 3, Lord Krishna says whatever actions of a great man will be followed by people in general:

In the end, we can talk about the side stories and how Sita was treated and what took place, but we must look at the lessons and teachings and use them in our lives. What is the point of talking about these things and how the importance of Women are in our lives if we do not implement it etc..? There are many versions of the Ramayana in which points can be taken, i.e. Adhyatma Ramayana states that Sita Knew she will be kidnapped by Ravana, and Ravana knew he would meet death at Shri Rama's hands etc. In the end, some say we should not look at the negative events that has happened to Sita, "its part of the Lila etc..", but this would be wrong, not everything is done for God's sake, its done for humanity's understanding. We must understand the events and relate it back to our society and ourselves. We must take the lessons and view women in our lives as that Divine Sita Devi.

Women Power

The Ramayana- the epic is still very much alive and permeates all aspects of our live from politics to reality television. In grandmother's generation there were lots and lots of women called

Sita in today generation. There is not a single Sita. Women, obviously, don't want to call their daughters Sita; why name their daughters after a long-suffering, abandoned, self-sacrificing wife? Women don't want that fate for their daughters. Sita's Ramayana came partly out of feeling the need to have a retelling of the Ramayana that gave Sita a voice. I think a lot of women who are single mothers, in tough situations, who are struggling to make a life for themselves in what is still very much a man's...world, can find inspiration in Sita's courage. We shouldn't forget the ending of the Ramayana as it is narrated in the Valmiki and many other versions-that Sita chooses, instead of returning to Ayodhya and being Rama's queen, to go back to where she came from the earth. She makes a choice; she strikes out on her own. It's a very powerful, proto-feminist choice. In the dilemmas that Rama and Sita face, we can find an echo of our own problems. There are episodes that aren't always neat, aren't black and white I think they should provoke us to think, engage with the text, and ask questions. If we cease to engage with the epic, we start to forget what a powerful and influential story it is.

The women's anguish is portrayed well: from Mandodari's pain to Tara's anguish on being asked to return to former husband Sugriva and also Rama's lashing out at Sita after his victory, when he says, "Sita, you are free. I have freed you. You can do whatever you want. Go wherever you want." Unfortunately, we live in a time that when you call something feminist, it immediately makes people think that it's only for women. So it is not proper to call it a feminist Ramayana for that reason it is really like little boys to go out and read this. Women, engagement with Sita and the Ramayana will be coloured by that and that's what identified with Mandodari, Tara and Sita. And the bit about Rama's conversation with Sita after his victory.

Both epics engages in different ways, and for different reasons. The Mahabharata is an epic that is always relevant someone once said that the Mahabharata is about war, and so it is relevant to every experience of conflict. Maggi Lidchi-Grassi, whose three-volume, The *Great Golden Sacrifice of the Mahabharata* came out recently, draws parallels between the Mahabharata and World War II. Dharamvir Bharati's play on the Mahabharata, *Andha Yug*, is influenced by Partition. When Peter Brook dramatised and filmed the Mahabharata in the 80's, his choice of an international cast showed that the epic is relevant to all cultures; it speaks to every experience of conflict, including Vietnam and the Cold War. Karna is a tragic hero, and his story and fate reveal that conflicts are always more complex and tragic, that the ideas of good-and evil aren't absolute and are very complex.

The way the epic has travelled outside India and evolved in Indonesia, a Muslim country, and in Buddhist Thailand is something we often neglect. It's a pan-Asian tradition, and the proliferation of the epic is fascinating. Every re-teller of the story has added a new nuance, and has a different perspective on the story. As for characters, Sita is fascinating. All the female characters, from Kaikeyi to Urmila and Surpanakha, intrigues.

When it comes to Indian women, the picture is largely unchanged; depressingly so, going by the World Development Report 2012, released by the Bank The latest report focusing on Gender Equality and Development makes dismal reading. No doubt, the lot of women in India has improved over the years but not commensurately with the progress made by their country. As a result, women today might be better off than their mothers but trail their counterparts, even in many developing countries, when it comes to basics such as survival, education, participation in the labour force and so on. As the report puts it, 'Despite stellar economic growth in recent years, maternal mortality (in India) is almost six times that in Sri Lanka.' Hardly the kind of statistic one would expect to read of a country that boasts of a woman President and has women at the helm of both the main ruling political party and the Opposition. But then-India has always been a land of contrasts and never more than when it comes to women. On the one hand, India has achieved, in 55 years, a decline in fertility comparable to what the US did in 100. On the other, gender inequalities persist in almost every sphere. Women earn less than men for comparable work, ownership of assets is distinctly skewed against them and participation in the labour force has been stagnant at little over 30% for more than three decades (the 66th round of NSSO seems to suggest a decline). The picture is not much brighter when one turns to other indicators such as sex ratios, health and education. About 22 % of the four million 'missing' women in the world are in India, damning evidence, if any were needed, of the limited success of laws in changing deeply-entrenched tradition.

The report advocates targeting the determinants of the gender gap rather than the outcomes, a suggestion well worth pursuing, given that past attempts focusing on outcomes have not delivered. Instead, reducing female mortality, removing gender gaps in education, improving access to economic opportunities, increasing women's voice and agency in society and limiting reproduction of gender inequality across generations, might.

7

Sita's Dilemma

Sita foresees danger in Rama's decision to eliminate the demons in Dandaka forest, without any provocation from their side, at the request of some sages. She narrates an old episode about a sage who in possession of a weapon became violent and cruel.

Sita addresses Rama with this percept. "Wielding weaponry you are entering into an area where the demons are dense, and you intolerantly embark to kill them, thereupon we two get separated, which in turn is intolerable to you. So let us leave weapons back at hermitage and go to forests to see sages-Govindaraja." The promise made to sages in eradicating demons is himsaatmaka, injurious; they can be won over by *ahimsa*, non-injurious methods also. None can avert Rama to make a promise, nor ask him to deviate.

There is an interesting juncture in Ramayana, where Sita reminds about the question of triggering cause for Rama's waging a war against demons. It is said there, that if Sita is said to be self-contradictory in telling Rama that bow and arrows are a must to Kshatriya-s to protect the helpless when saying 'safeguard the sufferers, then only Kshatriya-s should use their bow...' as at verse 3-9-26 and also questioning immediately at 3-9-27, 'where the Kshatriya dharma, where the hermit's way of living...' etc., She is not contradicting herself in her statements, but asking Rama to have a cause, without resorting to weaponry against those demons, in a straightforward way *atax tad rakyashya -yudhamna grhyam iti etad abhipr-yakatv-t* II.

She is inquisitive to know why Rama alone shall raise the bow and arrows against some demons hurting some sages. These sages are having super powers and Indra like celestial chiefs are coming to these sages to take them to heaven with their mortal bodies. Can't they eliminate these demons? But these super hermits are not going to heaven, which is the minimum ambition of any penance, but requesting Rama to protect them from demons. And Rama obligingly started to wage this unilateral war, where any war requires a triggering point. Can't the super sages eliminate these demons, with their powers acquired by their penances? This is the question of Sita. For this, Rama replies so convincingly in the next chapter, saying that the sages cannot issue forth a curse at the demons, in the course of their penance.

Sage Vishvamitra, though being a furious sage, once sought the help of Rama to counter the Demoness Tadaka. And Rama rendered it. Now also these sages do not waste their powers at the mischievous demons, but ask Rama to safeguard their interests, for Rama is the king, whether he may be in capital or in forests.

Secondly, Rama is subjected to the throne of Ayodhya, temporarily being held by his brother Bharata, and as a loyalist to that throne, Rama should act in accordance with the rules of his kingdom. This area Dandaka forests is under the ambit of their own kingdom. So Rama has to perform the deeds suitable to their kingdom. When killing Bali, Rama speaks to Bali – "all this area is under our kingdom, now held by Bharata, and it is my duty to act in accordance with the decree of that throne..."

"Regarding the cause, Sita's doubt comes true and she alone becomes the ultimate cause for Rama, to wage the final war with Ravana.

Ramayana-Jayant's misdeed and how Lord Rama punished him.

The verse in question is this-

"vaayasaH sahasaa utpatya vidadaara stana antare" || 5-67-3 (Valmiki Ramayana)

or

"vaayasaH sahasaagatya vidadaara stana antare"

"वायसः सहसागत्य विददार स्तनान्तरे"

The meaning of this, as written is that Jayant in the form of a crow attacks Mata Sita's chest. This sounds highly indecent. And the reason behind such translations is the improper description by Kalidas of this episode in the 12th *Sarga* of his Raghuvansh mahakavya. That indecent description has resulted in such translations being done today. Everything he says cannot be a *Pramaan*. He himself attests this- पुराणामित्येव न साधुसर्वे what is ancient need not necessarily be good.

So the need is to understand the meaning of the word "स्तन" in the above verse, with the help of Panini grammar. Shaktayana believes that the origin of each Sanskrit word lies in its *Dhaatu*. And Panini in a way also agrees with it. Now if we see "Siddhant Kaumudi", we will find that *Dhaatu* number 461 says "टन् *dhaatu* and वन *dhaatu* are used as the meaning of the word. They are षब्दार्थक धातु. And the word "Lru" originates from "टन्" *dhaatu*, as the मूर्धन्या" if used in the begining of a *dhaatu* becomes दन्त्य 'स'

So "स्तन" comes from "टन्" which is a षब्दार्थक धातु. So if someone says "मेधास्तनन्ति" it would mean the clouds are roaring. Similarly, oufUr flagknk;ks ;fLeu rn~ oua means where lions, etc roar is known as van (forest). Therefore "विददार स्तनांतरम" would relate to the foot of Sitaji in which she wears anklet. The word "स्तन" therefore means the foot. In ancient times, it was used for foot only due to the sound produced from anklet which was worn by ladies and also for the udder of a cow as milking produces sound in utensil/bucket. Thus, Valmikiji describes Jayant attacking the foot of Sitaji, not any other part of body.

The story of Rama throwing darbhai at Jayanta in the shape of a crow can be found in the Ramayana.

In Ashoka *vana*, Sita heard the voice of Hanumana with fear and looked up into the tree, and saw the monkey who was eloquent and humble, and his eyes glowed like golden fire. Hanumana came down out of the tree, ruddy-faced and humbly attired, and with joined palms spoke to Sita. Sita introduced herself to Hanumana and asked for news of Rama, and Hanumana informed her all that had befallen and spoke of Rama and Lakshmana. While Hanumana got a little closer, Sita was much afraid as she thought him to be Ravana in disguise. Hanumana tried his best to convince Sita that he was Rama's friend and at last when she saw the signet-ring, she got convinced, and she was glad and sorry at once. Glad to know that Rama was alive and well, and sorry for his grief.

Hanumana then suggested Sita to sit on his back so that he could carry her back from Lanka across the sea to Rama.

She praised his strength, but would not go with him, because she thought she might fall from his back into the sea, especially if the *rakshasas* followed them, and because she would not willingly touch any person other than Rama, and she also desired that the glory of her rescue and the destruction of the *rakshasas* should go to Lord Rama. Hanumana praised her modesty and wisdom, and asked for a token for Rama.

Then Sita told him of an adventure with a crow, known only to herself and Rama that had befallen long ago at Chitrakuta, and she gave Hanumana a jewel from her hair, and sent a message to Rama and Lakshmana, praying them to rescue her. Hanumana took the gem and, bowing to Sita, made ready to depart.

The crow, which we think a very agile bird, is in fact very scary bird. Subconsciously it thinks, it is under attack. There is sub story in Ramayana known as Jayant son of lndra, episode, to how and why crow became cockeyed. Jayant took the guise of Kakasura in the form of crow.

Name of crow in Sanskrit is Kaaka: The crow's only language is kaa kaa. Kaa means 'who is she' in Sanskrit. The crow seems to be only species which always says 'who is she?' 'who is she?'

Is this she? ls that she? or ls this Sita she?

Once upon a time, Rama and Sita were relaxing under a tree. Rama fell asleep on Sita's lap and she was busy admiring the flowers growing nearby. An *asura*, Kakasura, took the shape of a crow and started bothering Sita. lt cawed loudly, brushed against her with its wings and tried to startle her into disturbing Rama's sleep. Sita, that model of virtue (really, thank goodness for mythology no woman ought to be like that!!!) didn't stir, so that Rama's sleep wouldn't be disturbed. Finally the *asura*, annoyed, pecked Sita's chest. The sharp beak of the crow, drew blood. And still she didn't utter a cry. The blood from her body dripped on Rama's brow and he stirred from his sleep. "What's this?" he demanded of Sita.

When she told him about the crow, Rama picked up the *darba* grass growing nearby, and sent it as an arrow after the crow. Kakasura, got scared and tried to outrun the arrow. He ran for many days and many nights, around the world and into hell and heaven. And yet, the arrow never swerved from its target.

Finally, Kakasura fell at Brahma's feet and asked what he should do. Brahma said, "Rama's arrow once released must find its goal. It will never tire till it reaches you. You had best go and ask for Rama's forgiveness." And so, Kakasura begged for Rama's forgiveness. Rama said, "All right. The arrow will take away one eye for the grief you have caused my dear wife but your life will be spared. Henceforth you will only be able to see out of one eye."

And so, Kakasura loses one eye to Rama's arrow but saves his life. And the crow even today, you will see, cocks its head from side to side since it can only see from one eyeball!!

The event is mentioned in retrospect at a later stage when she recalls this to Hanumana who plays the role of a messenger between the devoted (divine) couple who were forced by circumstances to experience a term of separation.

Sita concern about Ram to Kill Demon

In the Aranya Kanda of the Valmiki Ramayan it is stated as- Sita foresees danger in Rama's decision to eliminate the demons in Dandaka forest, without any provocation from their side, at the request of some sages. She narrates an old episode about a sage who in possession of a weapon became violent and cruel. Sita addresses Rama with this percept. "Wielding weaponry you are entering into an area where the demons are dense, and you intolerantly embark to kill them, thereupon we two get separated, which in turn is intolerable to you. So let us leave weapons back at hermitage and go to forests to see sages - Govindaraja." The promise made to sages in eradicating demons is *himsaatmaka*, injurious; they can be won over by *ahimsa*, non-injurious methods also. None can avert Rama to make a promise, nor ask him to deviate from it. Aware of this stubbornness of Rama, her heart felt a foreboding, and that love-blind Sita started telling in a friendlily manner, in view of her friendship with Rama, that may disrupt soon. "Gross unjust will accrue to any in an abstruse way if his indulgence is enkindled merely by his own desire, and in this world it is possible to fend them off, to have a recourse to justness... The duty of a prince, which you are going to take-up in the wake of promise given to sages, i.e., killing demons, without a valid reason, that which is righteous to you, can be performed in a different way...' "Only three self-gratifications, the definite products of desire, are there: one is speaking fallacious utterances, which itself is worse, and worst than the other two malefic self-gratifications, where the other two are the fascination for other's wife, and the cruelness without enmity.... Sita is foretelling the triggering points in the course of Ramayana. The addictions or self-gratifying acts are defined as: Hunting, sleeping in daytime, abusing others, indulgence in women, three artistic impulses namely music, dance and drama, wasteful wandering, are the ten desire. Manu Smriti "The habit of telling specious words is not there with you in the past nor it will be there in future, oh, Raghava, then wherefrom the virtue-ruining desire for other's women can be there.... "Oh, king, earlier this vile desire for other's women is absent in you, nor it is there now, unobserved is such a desire in any corner of your heart oh, prince, for you are always interested in your own wife... "You are conscientious, adherent of truth, and obliging father's orders, and in you virtue and truth, nay everything is established in you... All this can possibly be shouldered by one with controlled senses, and oh, graceful one for a gaze, I am also aware of your sense control.... The compound *mahaabaahoshakyam* is also cleaved as *mahaa baaho a shakyam*, meaning that 'your attributes are impossible to be known even by the self-controlled sages, but they are known to me...' so says Sita. "That third tendency to torture others' lives without enmity, that which will usually be effectuated unwarily, has now suddenly chanced before you... "Intending to safeguard the sages you have promised the dwellers in Dandaka forest, oh, valiant one, that you would eliminate demons in a fight... Only in this respect you have started towards the well-known Dandaka forest along with your brother, and wielding bow and arrows...Then on seeing your starting my mind is apprehensively upset, on verily reflecting about your bearing there appears to be no beneficial good for you... In any way, Sita's contemplation is, "you abide by your oath given to sages, and thus kill the demons. But without a cause you do not proceed to eliminate. If a cause for quarrel is to be there, that will be due to me. If I become the cause and depart you, you cannot survive without me, for you are not a polygamist. So how all these factors like your promise, monogamy, and eliminating demons, can be resolved by you? Thus I am thinking along with the associated troubles which you are going to undergo..." Your going towards Dandaka forest is not delightful to me, I tell the cause for that and listen to it as I tell... Indeed on entering the forest along with your brother, and wielding bow and arrows, seeing the forest ramblers there, won't you deplete arrows on all of them... The bow of warrior and the fuel of a burning fire if available within their reach, they immensely enhance their strength... "Once upon a time, oh, dextrous one, there was a pious and true worded hermit in some merited forest that was wanted by animals and birds. Then Indra came to that hermitage handling a sword, and donning a soldier's guise, to cause hindrance to that hermit's ascesis... Indra gave that best sword to store, there in that hermitage to that sage who is lasting in his ascesis, on a redeemable basis.

"On receiving that sword, he who is duteous in guarding the entrustment, moved about in the forest always handling the sword, to safeguard the confidence reposed in him. Wherever that dedicated guardian of that entrustment goes, even to obtain tubers or fruits, he did not go without that sword. Carrying that sword always, that hermit slowly made his own faculty infuriated, loosing determination in ascesis. Then with the constant association of that weapon that sage gradually became inadvertent, and smitten by vice he went to hell. "Thus, all this happened earlier, only owing the reason of associating with a weapon constantly, and the sequel of constant association with weapon is as good as constant association with fire. In affinity and in respect I am reminding but not tutoring you, and in anyway improper is that thought of yours to wield your bow to kill the demons dwelling in Dandaka without any enmity, oh, brave one, undesirable is the killing of offenceless. For the valiant Kshatriya-s who are inclined in forests heartily, the purpose of the bow is this much 'safeguarding the sufferers...' Kshatriyas should delight in their class-oriented righteousness, even when in forests. Thus Sita's thinking is that they should live like hermits in forests, without resorting to the warring attributes of Kshatriya class. She further says that the function of bow is limited to safeguard the suffering lot...

Rama Replies

"Where that weapon? Where this forest? Where the principles of Kshatriya? And where is sageness? All this is inconsistent... let us esteem the laws of the land... Weapon admiring mind becomes maligned with avariciousness, you may therefore follow the tenet of Kshatriya-s on going to Ayodhya again... "Everlasting satisfaction will be there to my father-in-law and mothers-in-laws, on your becoming a devout sage even after forfeiture of kingdom... From virtuousness prosperity emanates, from righteousness happiness, and by honourableness all are achieved, and this universe is the essence of probity... Experts will make efforts to exhaust their own selves with those and those principles, thus they realise sublimity... unachievable is pleasure by pleasuring alone... "Always tread along the righteousness with a pure mind, oh, gentle one, and specially in these sagely forests... you know everything in all the three worlds, in all its nuances... I cite all this with my womanly waver, and who is capable to talk to you about dharma? Ponder mindfully along with your brother, and what that is appropriate, you do it...but not belatedly..."

This particular chapter is an interesting juncture in Ramayana, where Sita reminds about the question of triggering cause for Rama's waging a war against demons. Sita's doubt is well explained in *Dharmaakuutam*, the encyclopaedic commentary on Ramayana. It is said, that if Sita is said to be self-contradictory in telling Rama that bow and arrows are a must to Kshatriya-s to protect the helpless when saying 'safeguard the sufferers, then only Kshatriya-s should use their bow..." and also questioning immediately at 'where the Kshatriya dharma, where the hermit's way of living...' etc., *dharmaakuutam* says not so. She is not contradicting herself in her statements, but asking Rama to have a cause, without resorting to weaponry against those demons, in a straightforward way.

She is inquisitive to know why Rama alone shall raise the bow and arrows against some demons hurting some sages. These sages are having super powers and Indra like celestial chiefs are coming to these sages to take them to heaven with their mortal bodies. Can't they eliminate these demons? But these super hermits are not going to heaven, which is the minimum ambition of any penance, but requesting Rama to protect them from demons. And Rama obligingly started to wage this unilateral war, where any war requires a triggering point. Can't the super sages eliminate these demons, with their powers acquired by their penances? This is the question of Sita. For this, Rama replies so convincingly that the sages cannot issue forth a curse at the demons, in the course of their penance.

Sage Vishvamitra, though being a furious sage, once sought the help of Rama to counter the Demoness Tadaka. And Rama rendered it. Now also these sages do not waste their powers at the mischievous demons, but ask Rama to safeguard their interests, for Rama is the king, whether he may be in capital or in forests.

Secondly, Rama is subjected to the throne of Ayodhya, now being held by his brother Bharata, and as a loyalist to that throne, Rama should act in accordance with the rules of his kingdom. This area Dandaka forests is under the ambit of their own kingdom. So Rama has to perform the deeds suitable to their kingdom. When killing Bali, Rama speaks to Bali – "all this area is under our kingdom, now held by Bharata, and it is my duty to act in accordance with the decree of that throne..."

"Regarding the cause, Sita's doubt comes true and she alone becomes the ultimate cause for Rama, to wage the final war with Ravana.

8

Life Management Tips from the Life of Sita

Life is small and valuable, time is going fast any moment we are nearing death. Death never spare any one either rich or poor. Every individual is equal before death. It can come any time without any prior notice. We have finish maximum good work in minimum time. We have search souls who finishes maximum good work in minimum time at moderate cost. There should be proportionate return against energy consumed. There should be management of time to get maximum return. We must finish our work in a planned way. There should not be any laziness and carelessness. We must remember we are made answerable to every work what we have done.

Life of mother goddess indicates about the period and activity. The correct definition of life lies in these two words–time period and work. The life what we have got is definite block of period. We have to work and enjoy life in this limited period. In over present life we are allowed to do the activities as per our choice. But what we do in this present time in not limited to only present it also effects our activities already done in the past and will have effects on future activities. If anything wrong had been done in the past we can repent by doing good works and effects will be reflected in our future activities. Those who are aware of this facts indulges in only good works and his every moment is spent in thinking and doing only good works. They are fully aware that life is not meant for full filling desires and sex. But is only meant for doing good works. Those who are not aware of this fact wonders here and there. Sometimes they are trapped by desire and sex. We are free to do anything only to some extent. We can do anything as per our desire in our present but all these gets accumulated in future and are bound to reap the fruits as per their deeds.

Thus life is not only a period or activities but is the lively combination of both. Therefore people who are engaged in good work gets only good result. And those who are trapped in fulfilling wrong desires never gets good results. Thus we should protect ourselves from such bad thought and activities. Goddess mother is the regulator of this time and work. Therefore she is called as Mahakali. When she gives fruits of good work is called as Mahalakshmi and when she dispels wrong desire from our mind and pure it, is called Maha Saraswati. But Goddess Mahakali destroys those who are indulged in bad works and moves on wrong path. She captures all their prosperity.

Sita was born to remove the difficulties of people suffering from draught at that time and also to destroy the prosperity of proud king Ravana. Who was indulged only in bad works. Similarly, we also require a new Sita in present days to destroys the evil of corruption and pure our mind from bad thought.

Sita is an integral part of our psyche. At every stage of an Indian woman's life her name is invoked. Certain aspects of a character have been emphasized more than others to suit the political and societal norms of the day. Most have focused on the negative interpretations of Sita, not the positive. Ramayana is rarely understood as Ramcharitramanas, a character study of humans and emotions. In a world where the role of women is still being redefined Sita's character teaches us valuable lessons for the contemporary society.

Some see Sita as a *pati vrata*, the ideal woman. Some see her as victimized. Yet, others see a more liberated Sita, a cherished wife of Rama. She was outspoken, freely expressed herself, was tempted by the material golden deer, spoke harsh words, repented, loved her husband, was faithful to him, served her family, did not get seduced by the glamour and material objects in Ravana's palace, faced an angry and suspicious husband, tried to appease him, reconciled her marriage, later accepted her separation and raised well balanced children as a single mother.

Sita revealed her greatness wherever she was placed. It was not that the lives of Ramayana characters were so pure, free from human weaknesses and so divinely protective that no complicated situations could arise to upset them. The greatness consisted in their strength that truth, sincerity, self-sacrifice and other virtues gave. Sita's greatness was more pronounced, for she portrayed a greater power of endurance that any other character, except possibly Rama. Hers was not the endurance of the stone, with no outside expression for the inner workings. Hers was the special capacity, amidst the wailing and complaints to use her discrimination to face her challenges in a dignified manner.

In Ramayana, almost every great woman, like Mandodari. Shabri, Tara and others after the initial calamity from outside or from within, did produce the normal human reaction of feeling desperate. But as the first effects subsided, every woman regained her balance, until she reached the highest values of life that humankind can ever manifest under similar circumstances.

The greatness of most men and women consist in their strength than truth, similarly self-sacrifice and other virtues. If the test of greatness is the capacity to remain true to one's principles in spite of terrors and temptations, Sita's greatness was undoubtly more pronounced for she portrayed a greater power of endurance that any character except possibly Ram. It is not that Sita did not cry or complain. Hers was not the endurance of the stone or the wall with no outside expression for the inner working. Hers was the special capacity, amidst the wailing and complains to use her discrimination and to face her challenges in a dignified manner.

The Patua version of the Ramayana is an oral, folk tradition. The folk traditions are sung by women who have often express their feelings and oppressions of their own lives in the wonderful songs about Sita.

Women today are confronted by so many complex choices – as they try to juggle the demands thrust upon them as daughters, wives, mothers, career women. There is lot in common with the dilemmas present day women face and the choices and similarities that Sita had herself experienced. It is important to see Sita not as just a wife, or queen but as a women in her own right-and one who, at times in various retellings, displays a great of sensitivity, maturity and insight. At last she rejects Ram's offer to return to Ayodhya if she proves her virtue again. It is a powerful moment– She rejects returning to be a queen to a people who doubted her, rejects being a wife to a husband who abandoned her even though she was pregnant with his children. Through the ages many have been uncomfortable with that ending–is it a tragedy. She was right in rejecting the people who doubted her, she was right in rejecting her husband who did not care for her against his duties towards his subjects. But was she right in leaving her own children Lav and Kush without any fault. Of course, they became the prince of Ayodhya but without a lovely mother. The decision of Sita should not be seen a tragedy. She emerges as women in her own right with her own mind, making her own choices. She grasps and controls her own fate with that choice.

The story of Sita has always deeply troubled many lovers and devotee of the epic Ramayana, namely the unjust banishment of Sita in response to doubts on her chastity. She feels injustice in the treatment meted out to her. Sita's like, is a story of a women whose sense of righteousness is accompanied by an equally strong sense of comparison. Even as she despairs in the Ashoka grove and waits anxiously for her captivity to end, this is a Sita who can empathizes with the sufferings of others, including the *Rakshasis* who must lose their husbands in the war. In this comparison and empathy, ultimately, she emerges as a stronger than Rama, an unhappy man torn between love his wife and a sense of duty towards his subjects.

When referring to the *Ramayana*, the Vaishnava classic *Sri Vachana Bhushanam* fondly and reverently records: "The great *itihasa, Ramayana*, speaks of the nobility of the imprisoned lady." That is indeed the very essence of Valmiki's epic, the image of the imprisoned splendour, the epic of the Earth-born.

Sri Aurobindo has said "The work of Valmiki has been an agent of almost incalculable power in the moulding of the cultural mind of India, it has presented to it to be loved and imitated in figures like Rama and Sita, made so divinely and with such a revelation of reality as to become objects of enduring cult and worship, or like

Hanumana, Laksmnana, Bharata the living human image of its ethical ideas, it has fashioned much of what is best and sweetest in the national character, and it has evoked and fixed in it those finer and exquisite yet firm soul tones and that more delicate humanity of temperament which are a more valuable thing than the formal outsides of virtue and conduct."

When we read the *Ramayana* we do follow the life story of Rama –and a marvellous tale it is of ethical imperatives, war-heroism and awe-inspiring idealism. But it is Sita who stays back in our consciousness at the end. Sita brought to the marriage pandal by Janaka; Sita giving away her riches and preparing to follow Rama into the forest; Sita shyly recounting her marriage festivities to Anasuya; Sita charmed by the *Rishis* and *Rishipatnis*; Sita thrown into a fright by Viradha and Surpanakha; Sita demanding the golden deer and accusing Lakshmana; Sita abducted by Ravana and imprisoned in Lanka; Sita terrorised by the ogresses and consoled by Hanumana; Sita spurned at the very moment of victory but vindicated by the tire-ordeal; Sita anointed queen and gifting Hanumana a string of pearls; and, of course, the terrible fate that awaits her in the *Uttara Kanda*, and her withdrawal.

But nothing about the antecedents of Sita. She is shown as rising to the occasion at every moment of crisis. But we have not the same background knowledge about her as we have of Rama. But Sita has a passive role most of the time. She is on her own only in the Sundara Kanda. The birth and growth of Sita, her "world" within: of these Valmiki is mostly reticent. For instance, after her marriage, Janaka fades out of the story altogether. While Dasaratha, Kausalya, Sumitra, Kaikeyi and the brothers are a constant presence, we do not hear anything about Janaka, his queen and Sita's sisters. Indeed, except for the names Urmila, Mandavi and Srutakirti we have no idea of their lives, characters and relationship with Sita. It is mostly Rama's world in the *Ramayana* in spite of the fact that we are equally concerned with Sita's story of noble suffering. If Rama is the prince who became God. Sita too is a princess who became a goddess. But there what are the guiding pathways in her ascent to the summits? Devotees have linked Sita to the Supreme Mother seen severally as Sri Devi,

Bhu Devi and Sri Ranganayaki. Parasara Bhatta exclaims in *Sri Guna Ratna Kosa*: "The *Ramayana* lives because of you." he further says:

"O Mother who was born as Maithili! While Rama saved only those who surrendered to him, you saved even those who did not. Such is thy profound compassion."

And he says that the Sita incarnation was a rehearsal for the stage appearance as Sri Ranganayaki by Lakshmi Devi.

Poets and dramatists have also sought to approach the *Ramayana* events from Sita's point of view. Among the most significant creations in this genre in recent times is Kumaran Asan's *Chintavishtayaya* Sita (1919), As a remembrance of events past in Sita's life while she awaits the return of Lav and Kusa from Rama's court, the poem is almost bitter. How could one who showered so much affection upon her during the 13 years' exile become the stone-hearted crowned King of Ayodhya? Does power really corrupt people?

"It is hard to say it–Even a scamp would resent anyone slandering his wife. How then did the noble king heed as gospel truth the aspersions made against me?"

And yet the image of compassionate that Sita is, that she forgives Rama as easily as she forgave the ogresses in the Asoka grove. The ways of *Raja Dharma* are inscrutable! Hence she ends up blaming herself for her clouded vision:

"Lord, have mercy on your vainglorious mate!
pardon me for the blemishes
that in a state of mental disturbance
I discovered just now in you!"

Sita, born of earth, daughter of Mother Madhavi, is a symbol of us all, the earth-born, children of Mother Sakhambari. Sita's story speaks of the greatness of the lady who remained in an apparently vast and foliage-rich garden, but she was really imprisoned there by an unscrupulous *Rakshasa* monster, and constantly teased and terrified by ugly ogresses. Well, we too are on this earth, a vast garden limning the splendour of *Prakriti*. But we are also imprisoned by our own senses (*Karma* and *Jnana*

Indriyas) and are threatened by a variety of fate-made, man-impelled, self-created sicknesses. Sicknesses of the body and the mind. We are imprisoned by birth, imprisoned by the lust of others, imprisoned by our own longings. However, the imprisoned lady in Asoka was Sita, a Princess, a queen-to-be. We too may be pigmy humanity, but we are also *amrutasyah putrah*, children of immortality. Hence Valmiki took up the story of Sita to tell us what we are, whither we are going, what should be our goal.

Sita's instinctive reverence for *Rishipatnis* like Katyayani, Maitreyi, Arundhati, Ahalya and Anasuya gives a new direction to the story. With such realised women around, it is obvious that woman is no ignorant cog in a gigantic life-machine. If she still suffers, it is because of blind tradition and crass selfishness which have turned her into a blinded slave.

Sita is seen as a tremblingly human and graciously divine heroine. Her innocence and wisdom, gentleness and strength, love and compassion are all reflected in her motivations, conversations, and actions. When the moment of despair is upon us, and we feel helpless and hopeless in an increasingly menacing atmosphere, the image of Sita clad in the ochre robes of renunciation rises before us as a promise, guiding us to sanity, guarding us as Grace. And so the noble tale of Sita becomes our sanctuary as well.

Sita Desire to go to forest

In the Ayodhya Kand of the Valmiki Ramayan it is stated as:

bhartur bhaagyam tu bhaaryaa ekaa praapnoti purusa risabha |

atah caiva aham aadistaa vane vastavyam iti api || 2-27-4

"Oh, Rama the best of men! Wife for one gets fortune of the husband. For that reason, I am also destined to dwell in the forest."

na pitaa na aatmajo na aatmaa na maataa na sakhii janaH |

iha pretya ca naariiNaam patir eko gatiH sadaa || 2-27-5

"To a woman, father or son or self or mother or female companion are not the recourse. Husband alone is forever the best recourse either in this world or after her death."

If you set forth now itself to the forest, which is difficult to be travelled, I shall come before you, by trampling down thorns and grass with long pointed stalks."

"Oh, brave man! By abandoning, as water left over after drinking, the impatience and anger and having faith, take me. There is no sin in me." She said, "Protection under the feet of the husband is better than being on top of a lofty building or in aerial cars or in moving through the sky or in attaining all types of positions." "My mother and father taught me of different matters long ago. I need not be told now, how to deal in any way with anyone." "I can come to forest which is inaccessible, which is devoid of people, filled with various types of animals and inhaited by tigers and jackals." "Not thinking of three world, thinking of loyalty to husband, I shall dwell in the forest happily as though staying in our father's house." Performing service to you regularly, having the necessary discipline, observing chastity, I would like to stay with you in the forests which smell like honey." Here in the forest, you are indeed capable of protecting other people also. Why to tell about my protection?" "Today no doubt, I will come to forest along with you. Oh, the illustrious! I, with this intention, cannot be prevented to do so." I shall live only on roots and fruits always, no doubt. Living along with you, I shall not create any unpleasantness to you. "With you the learned and the lord, I shall not have fear anywhere. I wish to see rivers, mountains, small lakes and grooves." I shall be comfortable, by coming together with you, the courageous man. I desire to see lotus-ponds filled with swans, water-fowls and excellently flowered. "Oh, the large eyed lord! Remaining dedicated to you, I shall take bath regularly in those lakes and with full of joy, I shall sport with you." Thus spending even a hundred thousand years in your company I shall never find any deviation/ Heaven also will not be acceptable to me otherwise. Even if in heaven there is residence for me without you, I do not like it. I shall proceed to the forest, which is very much inaccessible and occupied by monkeys, elephants as well as other animals. Clining to your feet alone, I shall dwell in the forest as though in father's home. "Therefore, grant well my prayer and usher me-me without any other thought, whose mind is fondly attached to you and who am determined to die if separated from you. Due to this, there will be no burden to you from me." Sita along with him even thought she was speaking as a foresaid. To hold her back from coming to forest, he also started talking highly of the various afflictions she might have to face in a forest. Rama describes various troubles of staying in forest and beseeches Sita not to go to forest.

Rama Warns about Difficulties of Staying in Forest

Thinking of difficulties one will be called upon to bear in the forest, Rama who was fond of righteousness did not form the idea of taking Sita who was speaking as aforesaid.

Soothening with kind words to Sita, when eyes were blemished with tears, the virtuous Rama spoke again as follows, for the purpose of waking her turn back.

You are born in a high lineage, ever devoted to righteousness. Perform your own virtue here, which is agreeable to my mind. "Do whatever I tell you. There are many inconveniences in the forest. Know them from me." "Oh, Sita! Let your thought made about forest be given up. It is indeed said that forest with its wilderness is fraught with many dangers." "Anger and greed are to be abandoned by the dwellers of forest. Devotion is to be bestowed on asceticism. What needs to be feared, should not be feared. Hence, living in a forest is a suffering." "Therefore, do away with the idea of your coming to the forest. Forest is not indeed bearable for you. Reflecting now, I perceive forest as having too many disadvantages." As the great souled Rama did not agree to take her to the forest, the much aggrieved - Sita implores upon Rama to allow her to come to forests, and says that she heard through some foretellers that she has to live in forests for some time, when she was with her father's place. But Rama is not interested to make Sita's life penurious in forests and once again tries to pacify her. He asks her to stay back at Ayodhya. For that Sita laments to become lonely parted with her husband.

Sita Insists on Going to Forest

Sita was distressed to hear these words of Rama and spoke these words slowly, with her face with tears.

"know all those disadvantages you mentioned about dwelling in the forest become advantages to me, if your affection is placed before them." Antelopes, lions, elephants, tigers, *sarabhas* (legendary animal with eight legs), birds, yaks and all others which roam in the forest, run away after seeing your form, since they have never seen your figure before. When there is cause for fear, who would not have fear? "As per the command of the elders, I also should go along with you. My life is to be abandoned here, if I were separated from you." "Even Devendra the Lord of celestials, by his strength, cannot over power me, who is in your vicinity." "I shall be the one who has fulfilled the *brahmana's* word. I shall accompany you to the forest. The time has come for *brahmana's* words to come true." Even though she requested him in many ways about setting out to the forest, he did not agree to take her to the forest, which is a solitary place. After hearing Rama's words, Sita was sorrowful, moistening with earth as it were with burning tears, trickling down her eyes. Rama the prudent man then pacified in many ways, to avert that Sita with red lips, who was sorrowful as above, cute-cloths that are befitting to sages and saints are brought in for the three at the behest of Kaikeyi. Rama and Lakshmana accept and wear them. But Sita, as a par excellent princess of Mithila, is baffled in wearing them and when she is irksome as how to tie and toggle them, Rama goes to her and demonstrates how to wear them, on her silken robes. Seeing that situation, all the womenfolk in the palace chamber wail for the hardship befallen on Sita.

Kaikeyi Offer Tree Bark to Sita

Thereupon, Kaikeyi shamelessly bringing personally of men, said to Rama; "Put these on" Taking those two pieces of bark (as loin cloth and cover) from kaikeyi and discarding his clothing of fine yarn, Rama put on the garb of ascetics. Lakshmana too there itself before his father put on the clothing of ascetics, by discarding his beautiful raiment. Then, Sita who wore silken clothing, by seeing the piece of bark intended to be worne by her, felt alarming as a deer would on seeing a snare (set for entrapping). Feeling abashed while taking the wearing apparel made of *Kusa* grass and greatly troubled in mind, Sita who bore auspicious marks knew what is righteousness who was an illustration of righteousness spoke these words with her eyes filled with tears to her husband who looked like Chitraratha (the king of Gandharvas).

Sage Vashista Said to Kaikeyi

Thereafter, singly you alone with bad conduct hurt to people, rule this earth which is bereft of people and desolate, with its trees alone remaining. "Where Rama is not a king, that place will not indeed become on kingdom. That forest, where Rama will be living, can become a kingdom." "If Bharata is born to king Dasaratha, he is not fit either to rule the earth that is not being offered by his father nor to live as a son in your case." "Even if you can jump from the surface of the earth to the sky, Bharata who knows the record of his father's dynasty will not do as you wish him to do" "therefore, an unfriendly act (alone) has been done by you, even though you are covetons towards his well-being. There is none indeed in this world who is not devoted to Rama" "Oh, Kaikeyi! You will see now itself that beasts, elephants, deers and birds going with Rama and trees also turning their faces towards Rama." "Moreover, putting aside the bark of trees, give excellent jewellery to your daughter-in-law, Oh, Kaikeyi! the bark of trees is not ordained for her". Thus saying so, Vasishta prevented that wearing of garment by Sita. "Oh, Kaikeyi! It was solicited by you, the dwelling in the forest of Rama only. Let Sita, to be decorated daily, be adorned with ornaments and live in the forest along with Rama." "Let Sita go with excellent conveyances, well accompanied by attendants, with all costumes and useful accessories. Her exile was not indeed solicited by you, while asking for boons". Eventhough Vashishta, the preceptor of the king, who had an influence beyond compare and the best of *brahmanas* was speaking as above, Sita did not turn away here resolution to follow the ways of her beloved husband.

Anasuya Instructions to Sita

Sita agrees to the instructions given by Anasuya on the duties of a devoted wife. At the end of the conversation with Sita, Anasuya requests her to ask for a boon, and highly pleased with her, Anasuya bestows heavenly flowers and ornaments on her. Anasuya then requests Sita to relate to her the story of her marriage with Rama. Then Sita relates that story to Anasuya in detail.

"It is not a surprise that a venerable woman like a you, talk to me like this, for, I know well that a husband is a respectable person for a woman." "O, venerable woman! Even if my husband be without fortune, he should unhesitatingly be obeyed by me." "How much more, if he be renowned for his virtues, compassionate, master of my heart, who is ever affectionate, a religious person, manifests the tenderness of a mother and a father to me." "The exceedingly strong Rama bears himself to all other Queens, as he exercises his behaviour towards his mother, Kausalya." "The valiant and pious Rama who is devoted to Dasaratha and free from all sense of importance treats all those women as his mothers on whom Dasaratha has even once bestowed a single glance." I was given thus to rama in that *Svayamvara*, a process of self-choosing marriage. I became devoted, by my good works, to my husband who is excellent among men of strength.

Sita and Surpanakha

Sita and Surpanakha exemplify two types of women who appear almost universally in folklore and mythology: Sita is good, pure, light, auspicious, and subordinate, whereas Surpanakha is evil, impure, dark, inauspicious, and insubordinate. Although male characters also divide into good and bad, the split between women is far more pronounced and is always expressed in terms of sexuality. Similarly, when a woman such as Surpanakha performs a wrong deed, it is typically ascribed to her female nature, whereas Ravana's evil deeds, for example, are never said to spring from his male nature. It is also worth noting that in the *bhakti*-oriented Ramayanas, in which the evil-doings of the male characters are recast as devotional acts leading to eventual salvation, Surpanakha's salvation is not mentioned.

Sita is the chaste good woman; Surpanakha the "loose" bad woman. The good woman is one who remains controlled, both mentally and physically, by her husband (or, in his absence, her father, brother, or son) and whose sexuality is channeled into child-bearing and service to her husband. The scriptures make frequent references to a man's duty to unite himself with such a woman in order to produce sons and thereby fulfill obligations to the ancestors. According to an oft-quoted injunction, a woman must obey and be protected by her father in youth, her husband in married life, and her sons in old age; a woman should never be independent (Manusmrti V.147, IX.3). The good woman, however, is far from weak and powerless. She is a source of power, *Shakti*. In other words, it is her auspiciousness and nurturing that keep things going, but her power must be controlled to suit the purposes of a patriarchal society. Thus Sita comes to the forest as a companion to her husband, and she is watched over and protected every step of the way. Otherwise, she would not be allowed to set foot out of the palace.

The bad woman is one who is not subject to these controls. In contrast to Sita, Surpanakha is unattached and wanders about freely. In Valmiki, she describes herself as a strong woman who goes where she likes under her own power. It is not surprising that she is said to be a widow, since widows were considered dangerous and inauspicious, circumstances having rendered them unable to bear children. Her chastity was also suspect, since they were no longer under the control of a husband, and women were believed to have insatiable sexual appetites. In Hindi the word *suhagin* or *sumangali*, signifying auspiciousness, is used for a married woman whose husband is alive, Surpanakha's unmarried state is thus the major source of her evil nature; being a *raksasi* is at best a contributing factor. After all, Mandodari, also a *raksasi*, is praised for her virtue, chastity, and devotion to her husband, Ravana. Accordingly, it is Surpanakha's status as an independent woman which is denounced. But the loose woman, while perceived as dangerous, also holds a certain fascination for the male imagination, which is perhaps why Rama and Lakshmana linger a bit, egging her on rather than banishing her immediately.

It is revealing that Rama uses Sita as the excuse for Surpanakha's mutilation: the "bad woman" is punished in order to protect the "good woman," or perhaps to serve as an example of what would happen to the "good woman" if she decided to go "bad"—for the division of women into two types in fact reflects a basic mistrust of all women. One could even argue that if the beautiful and virtuous Sita is Laksmi, the goddess of prosperity and auspiciousness, then the ugly and unvirtuous Surpanakha must be her sister Alaksmi, the goddess of misfortune and inauspiciousness. In festivals honoring Laksmi, her sister Alaksmi is often driven away by lighting lamps, but in a Bengali Laksmi festival, an image of Alaksmi is made and ritually disfigured by cutting off its nose and ears, after which an image of Laksmi is installed in order to ensure good luck and prosperity in the coming year. The structural similarity between this popular ritual and the Surpanakha episode is striking.

The analysis of a single episode as it appears in selected tellings and interpretations can thus provide a telling glimpse into the dynamics of the Ramayana as a whole. The mutilation of Surpanakha is significant to the Rama story from multiple perspectives. From a narrative point of view, it serves as the catalyst for the key events: only after Surpanakha reports her disfigurement to Ravana does he decide to abduct Sita. From an ethical point of view, the episode raises complex questions about Rama's supposedly exemplary character, questions which authors and commentators have attempted to resolve in diverse ways. From a cultural perspective, the episode sheds light on Hindu attitudes toward female sexuality and its relationship to such polarities as good and evil, pure and impure, auspicious and inauspicious. However, the final word on Surpanakha has not been voiced: her story is sure to fascinate and inspire hearers, tellers, and interpreters for generations to come.

Ravana

"First, believe in this world," Swami Vivekananda said. The charismatic spiritual leader, believed that everything in the world was laden with meaning; with elements of Truth (*Satyam*), Holiness (*Shivam*) and Beauty (*Sundaram*). Swami Vivekananda said, "If you see something evil, think that you do not understand it in the right light."

"Throw the burden on yourself," he exhorted: do not play the blame game. This could explain why Rabindranath Tagore implored the writer Romain Rolland to study Vivekananda if he (Rolland) wanted to understand India. "(For) in him (Vivekananda), everything is positive and nothing negative!" Gurudev Tagore said. Nor did Vivekananda simply negate negativity. His view that even evil or negativity could be put to good use had revolutionary implications. Psychologist Oliver Burkeman tackles some of these from an opposite end of the ideological spectrum.

In Antidote: Happiness for Those Who Can't Stand Positive Thinking, Burkeman says most of us go through life under the delusion that it is certain people, situations or events that make us sad, anxious or angry. But when you look closely at your experience, you will be forced to conclude, as did the Stoic philosophers (and Vivekananda), that neither of these external events is 'negative' in itself. "Indeed, nothing outside your own mind can properly be described as negative or positive at all: what actually causes suffering are the beliefs you hold about those things."

The Rishi's complain to Brahama O Bhagavan! A *rakshasa* named Ravana, with your blessings, by his valour, is troubling all of us. We are not able to control him. Out of regard for the boons that you have given him we forgive all his actions. The sun cannot heat him, the winds cannot move him and the ocean does not 'tremble' any waves. He wishes to show up (*pradarshayitum*) *Sakra* (Indra) of the thirty kings (*tridasa rajanaam*). That bad minded one is the hater of the three worlds (*triin lokaan ucChitraan*). *(The Andhras had 30 walled cities prior to Megasthanes' visit to India and he mentioned them).*

अहो रूपमहो धैर्यमहोत्सवं महाधुतिः।

अहो राक्षसराजस्य सर्वलक्षणयुक्तता।।

(Aho roopmaho dheryamahotsavam mahadhutih

Aho raksharajasya sarvlakshnayuktta)

In the Valmiki Ramayan it has been said that if the irreligion had not over powered Ravana with beauty, patience, courage, he would have been even the king of the Gods.

Ravana was very learned and used to worship Lord Shiva. Ravana gave lesion to Rama on his death bed- "Things that are bad for you seduce you easily. You run towards them impatiently. But things that are good for you fail to attract you. You sheer them creatively, finding excuses to justify your procrastination. That is why I was impatient to abduct Sita but procrastinated in meeting you. This is the wisdom of life."

Ravana is worshipped in some places in Madhya Pradesh. Ravana's mother was Kaikasi and her mother was Ketumati. Ketumati's mother was a gandharva lady called Narmada. "A small temple to Ravana in Vidisha district's Ravangram village will echoes with the prayer, "Ravana Baba Namah" at Dusshera. The temple has an ancient idol of Ravana in a reclining position believed to have been constructed between the ninth and 14th century. The villagers believe it would be a bad omen to have the 10-foot idol stand erect and say that whenever this was done, some unexpected incident had occurred in the district. He has been worshipped as a symbol of prosperity for over 600 years by Kanyakubja Brahmins, a Brahmin sub-sect to which Ravana was believed to have belonged....Ravana is also worshiped in Ravana Rundi in Mandsaur district and Shajapur district's Bhadkhedi. In Mandsaur town, members belonging to the Namdeo Vaishnav Samaj, a Hindu sect, who worship the demon king on Dussehra, believe Ravana's wife Mandodari belonged to the town and they regard him as a son-in-law. A 35-foot high 10-headed Ravana statue was installed in 2005 at Ravana Rundi in the Khanpur area of Mandsaur....A 25-foot high lime and brick ancient idol of Ravana existed there till 1982. It developed cracks due to lightning and was ultimately destroyed.... The idol is worshipped every year and women in the area remain behind the veil on Dussehra since they regard Ravana as their son-in-law, while men make offerings at his statue if their wishes came true...Ravana and his son Meghnad are similarly worshipped at Bhadkhedi village in Shajapur district of western Madhya Pradesh... In Rajasthan's Hadauti village, while Gond tribals of Chhattisgarh also have a tradition of worshipping 'Lankapati (King of Lanka)..."

Himachal Pradesh Town: "Explaining the rationale for not celebrating Dussehra in Baijnath, Prem Parshad Pandit, member secretary of the high-powered committee of Himachal temples, told that the residents of Baijnath believe that participating in the celebrations means inviting the wrath of Lord Shiva. .." People believe that Baijnath is the place where Ravana meditated for years to appease Lord Shiva. As a result, Lord Shiva does not want his devotees to burn Ravana's effigy."

"Ravan Samhita is an astrological text or scripture narrated by lord Shiva and written by Ravana. Ravan Sanhita is the testimony to his great astrological knowledge and is considered as the standard book of reference.

Sita's Reply to Ravana

Sita replies to Ravana saying that He should seek friendship with Rama and return Her back to Rama. Sita listening to that horrible ogre's word, being tormented spoke in reply with a pitiable voice, pitifully and slowly. Being tormented by grief, in a pitiful state, with excellent limbs, devoted to husband, thinking about husband alone, with pleasant smiles Sita was sobbing, shivering and placing a straw in between herself and Ravana spoke thus in reply. "Turn your mind back from me. Let your mind be made on your own wives. Like best emancipation for a sinner, it is not appropriate to pray me. I was born in a great family. Getting such family, having one husband, a bad deed which is blamable is not to be made by me." Sita with renown thus speaking to that Ravana, turned back and spoke words again: "Like tiger by dog, smelling the scent of Rama and Lakshmana it is indeed not possible by you to stand in their view. To you like that, enmity with those two is like the enmity of one hand of Vruttasura with two hands of Indra and it is not persevering for you to be an opponent with them." "My husband that Rama together with Lakshmana will take away with His arrows your life quickly like the sun drying up shallow water. Killed by time even if you go to the mountain of Kubera or to his house or if you go to the assembly of King Varuna, without doubt you will not be released from Rama like a great tree from thunderbolt." Sita asks Hanumana, who is prepared to depart with the jewel for her head, to convey her enquiries about the welfare of Rama, Lakshmana and Sugreeva. She further requests Hanumana to urge them to rescue her. Then, Sita expresses her doubt about the capacity of Rama, Lakshmana and the troops of monkeys and bears to cross the ocean. Hanumana explains to Sita about the strength of monkey-heroes and assures her about their ability to cross the ocean. In the end, Hanumana consoles Sita by promising to bring Rama and Lakshmana on his back across the sea so that they will together destroy the City of Lanka.

Sita to Urge Rama and Lakshmana

Then, after giving the jewel for head, Sita spoke to Hanumana as follows: "This token of remembrance is actually known to Rama. By seeing this jewel, the heroic Rama can recollect three of us, viz. my mother, myself and the king Dasaratha. O Hanumana the excellent among monkeys! Driven by your enthusiasm again, think what remains to be done in undertaking this task. O Hanumana the best among monkeys! You are capable of fulfilling this task. O Hanumana! Become the one who can remove my misfortunes, by employing your effort. If you think of it carefully, your effort will become the one which can remove my misfortunes. "That Hanumana of terrific prowess, having promised 'so be it', offered salutation to Sita by bowing his head to her and was set off to go. Getting to know Hanumana ready to set out, Sita the princess spoke the following words with her voice choked by tears: "O Hanumana, the excellent among monkeys! Ask about the welfare of both Rama and Lakshmana together. You also ask, according to our usage, about the welfare of Sugreeva together with his ministers and of all the monkeys who are elder. You deserve to evolve a strategy through which the long-armed Rama can make me to cross over this ocean of misfortunes." "O Hanumana! Tell, in whatever manner, by which the illustrious Rama can console me, even while I am still surviving. Reap righteousness, by helping me through your word. "You can see soon those valiant monkeys, with their claws and tusks as weapons, having the prowess of lions and tigers and looking like lordly elephants, coming together." "O venerable lady! You shall see many troops of excellent monkeys resembling hills and clouds, thundering on the peaks of Malaya mountain in Lanka." "Hit in the vitals by the darts of venerable Manmatha the god of love, Rama is not obtaining happiness, as an elephant gets tormented by a lion." "O Sita the princess! Do not weep with grief. Let your mind be without any unpleasantness. You are indeed having Rama your husband as your protector like Shachi having Indra her husband as a protector." "Who else is there greater than Rama or who else equal to Lakshmana? Those two brothers, like fire and wind, are supportive to you." "O Sita the princess! You will not stay for long at this place, which is very terrific and occupied with a multitude of demons. The arrival of your husband will not be delayed. Be patient till the moment of my meeting with Rama on my return."

Sita Rebukes Lakshmana

This is a much debated in Ramayana because human complexities are involved in its narration. The sublimity of Sita's characterisation is disputed by her speeches in here. The question is whether Sita becomes an ideal woman in view of her tongue-lashing, or not. This is as good as asking the nature as to 'why it thunders before a storm, scaring children, birds and calves... cannot it just shower some rains and go...' If anything is not done in accordance with her wish and whim, or which goes against her peculiar way of thinking, it is usual for a shrewd woman to tongue-lash. Here, Sita is called a woman who is *bhart prema antha - bhart kÿema arthi* 'blinded by the devotement to her husband...' 'a desirer of her husband's welfare...' even at her own risk.

Thus this epic is called *ram ramayo ayanam ramyaoam* 'the peregrination of Sita and Rama...' where the first word Raamaa with elongated end syllable belongs to Sita and the second Raama with shortened end syllable belongs to Rama, and thus this is the peregrination of both Raamaa and Raama. If the course of the legend has to move forward, the characters have to move, and if they were to move, some situations should become turning points, and this is one such situation occasioned through the shrewdness of Sita. In a legendary perspective, if evil is to be eliminated, good has to peregrinate troublesomely, and that troublesome peregrination of Sita, as well as that of Rama, is triggered off at this situation, again due to the shrewdness of Sita. Thus, there is no oddity in the shrewd talk of Sita. Some more discussion is incorporated in the endnote. On identifying the grievous voice that is identifiable with her husband's voice, Sita spoke to Lakshmana, "you go at once, and check up on *Raghava*. I have heard the loud yelling voice of highly fretful Rama whereby my heart, or my very entity, is not abiding in its place, and it will be apt of you to protect such a brother of yours who is screaming in the forest. "He might have come under the subjugation of demons as with a bull coming under the seize of lions, hence, you hurry up so as to near such a brother of yours who is seeking protection." So said Sita to Lakshmana. Although she spoke a lot to him in this way, Lakshmana on his part has not moved out remembering his brother's order to stay guard to Sita, and hence that Janaki, the daughter of Janaka, who is already agitated for Rama further spoke to him in the paradox of his not going out of hermitage. "You are like a foe of your brother in friend's mien, Soumitri, as you are not making a move towards a brother even if he is in an emergency. Because of me you wish Rama to be completely destroyed, and only because of your cupidity for me you are not following up on Raghava. It is definite. The 'real' woman in Sita is coming out. From now on, she goes on talking unhesitatingly, unilaterally and even abusively because her mind is fuddled with the thought 'some damage is being done to her husband.' "'*Raghava* in direst strait' is the most liked thing to you, thus I deem, as you have no heart for that brother, and as you complacently stay behind even when that great-resplendent Rama is unseen. After which helmsman you have come here that Rama is undergoing an uncertainty of life-and-death, as such I indeed wonder what business you have here now in staying with me at this hermitage?" Sita spoke so to Lakshmana. Lakshmana spoke to Sita, the princess from Videha kingdom, who is talking deluged under tears and anguish in that way, as she is fretful like a she-deer. "Oh, Vaidehi, your husband is an impossible one for vincibility by serpents, *asura-s*, *gandharva-s*, gods, friends, demons, no doubt about it. Lakshmana is repeatedly addressing Sita as 'a broad-eyed-lady,' suggesting that 'though you have broad-eyes, but your mental perception is not that broad' 'as your eyes are belying your faculties.' 'And as 'the daughter of Janaka,' that is the 'daughter of a judicious person, yet unable to discriminate.' And as Vaidehi that is, one 'coming from Videha province.' Videha also means 'without body.' You are some supernatural, yet that demon beguiled you,' so on. Lakshmana said Sita 'be lost in desolation...' in the first instance and further said that she 'be blest...' and seeks the help of pastoral divinities to protect Sita in his absence. This appears self-contradictory on the part of Lakshmana. But it is held correct, for he uttered derogatory words in the first instance as a vexed person and then, on knowing what that is suddenly uttered by him, he is correcting himself in saying that 'she be blest...' He wished her to prosper as she belongs to Rama. Whatever belongs to Rama that cannot be ridiculed, especially his mother-like elder sister-in-law. The role of women in bringing alterations in joint families, peaceful histories or even in transcending legends is evident in every culture. *mahnto cpi hi bhidyante strybhi adbhi iva acal | kmandaka - lavaoa jalnt radya stry bhedntni bandhu hdayni | prcyna smti - dk* – 'They, the women, may be great beings but they tear asunder hearts, like oceans tearing great mountains.' Lakshmana is not eye-to-eye with Sita and he is going on listening all her accusations with his two ears. And in between his two ears his conscience is there which is not permitting him to tolerate these words, yet he is tolerating. With regard to touching another man, some texts say the word *kadaapi* 'never' and some *padaa api* 'by foot, even.' 'I do not touch any other man even with my foot.' This signifies 'marriage.' In marriages there is a custom for the newly-weds, like handshake and pressing toes of one another, in order to acclimatise one with the other's body touch. Here, if this *paadaa api* is taken as that custom in marriages. Thus she says that 'in the process of marriages such foot-pressing of bride and bridegroom occurs, hence I do not wish to undergo such situations.' As such, this is not mere touching someone with her foot. These intimidations of Sita that she will commit suicide by consuming poison, hanging, plunging in river, self-immolation etc., are not new to Sita or to any woman, under these irksome situations. She is giving many alternatives for suicide and the last one is self-immolation. If she is not going to die by hanging herself, or by consuming poison, or by drowning in river, then the question of self-immolation comes up. But she lists all of them in her anguish for Rama. With the same impetuosity she jumps into fire in the episode of *agni praveshanam* after war, when Rama belittles her. There also, she orders the very same Lakshmana to arrange pyre for her, disregarding her own accusations made at Lakshmana, at this situation. Till now Lakshmana is at her behind or at her sideways, as he usually stands a foot behind Rama or Sita, and now came to her fore to revere her *vis-à-vis* and made a semi-salute, i.e., briefly and briskly adjoined and disjoined his palms, without bringing the joined palms up to his heart or his face. Bringing the folded palms up to one's own heart is suggestive of 'pouring forth one's own heart' at the other, which is known in prayers as *iungo manus ante pectus* and if it is lifted up to forehead, it is suggestive of 'concentrating with whole of the mind,' and if hands are totally lifted into air it is for the god unknown. But here this *iungere manus*is neither *ante pectus, infra pectus,* nor *supra abdomen* but a quick gesture. He is performing *an iSTa namaskaara* 'un, interested, greeting...' 'a half-hearted gesture' like a 'cold-handshake' rather than a 'warm' one because he is now sent by her compulsively and compulsorily. 'When my fate is against me, and when my earlier sins [of finding fault with Lakshmana,] have acquired this [incarceration in Lanka...] one has to reap the results of one's own faults... a sinner, or a do-gooder, or one undergoing a capital punishment shall be treated kindly... who is he/she that does not offend...'

These are the very same words of Sugreeva in *Kishkindha*, Ch. 36, verse 11: "Either in faith or in friendliness if I have overstepped, in the least, that may be pardoned for I am an attendant of yours... for, none is unoffending...' All this culminates into the saying 'to err is human...'"

On the other hand, in the perspective of mythology, the time has come for Sita to go to Lanka, in order to effectuate her curse to Ravana as Vedavati, where Vedavati cursed Ravana, 'I will be the root cause for your total elimination... as Sita...' For such a transit, Rama shall go away from her, for that she wanted that golden deer and as a good husband Rama ran after it. But this security guard is an obstinate obstacle than Rama and he will not go away from here, because he has to keep custody of his brother's entrustment. Unless such unbearable words are spoken to a self-respectful person like Lakshmana, he does not stir out. To stop his leeching onto her, she had to talk in an abnormal way, which made him to go away, though reluctantly, and which paved the way for Ravana's entry. If the Golden Deer is not there, Rama will not go, if Rama's voice is not heard Lakshmana cannot be sent, and if Lakshmana does not go, Ravana will not come... then a blemish called anavasth˜ doÿa — ad infintum... occurs to Ramayana. If we do not mind to end Ramayana in that way, Ravana will be ruling high, even today...

Ravana Priases Sita's Beauty

Ravana praises Sita's beauty by extolling every limb of hers, though he enters like a Brahman *sanyaasi*, a friar. He indulges in a most untoward laudation that is unbefitting for a saintly and elderly almsman. Unable to refute him, because he is in such a pious garb, she had to invite him as an untimely guest. *Raghava's* younger brother Lakshmana is very much infuriated at Sita who spoke to him rudely, as such he journeyed towards Rama at once as though he is yearning to see Rama immediately, albeit his heart wanted him to stand guard to Sita. Quickly taking hold of intervallic time then the ten-headed Ravana approached Vaidehi adopting an aspect of a *sanyaasi*, a meandering Brahman friar. That *sanyaasi* is now cloaked in smooth silky saffron, his head-hair is neatly tufted, sandals are wooden, umbrella is on right shoulder, and on his left shoulder a shaft of *sanyaasi* is shouldered, onto which his handy water vessel is hooked, and he proceeded towards Vaidehi in a mien of meandering *sanyaasi*. There are many dress rules to a *sanyaasi* 'the Hindu sanyaasi' where the main items are, as said by Sage Angiirasa: *brahma stram tridanýam ca vastram jantu nivraõam | þikyam ptram bsym caiva kaupynam kai veÿitam* 'sacred thread, three-shafts, saffron clothing, deerskin, handy water vessel, grass-mat, loin-cloth, girdle-cloth... by these he will be known as a real *sanyasi* 'Hindu sanyaasi.' Out of all these items, the shafts make a difference. Vaishnavaite *sanyaasi-s* handle three shafts tied into one, and the three are symbolic to *cit, acit, iishvara* 'animate, inanimate, and lord...' and on this Manu says *vk daõýa ca mano daõýa kya daõýa tathaiva ca | yasya ete nihit buddhau sa tridaõýy ca ucya te* the word *danda* means 'repressing, suppression, control...' thus a *sanyaasi* has to control his 'speech, mind, and body... by that alone he is renowned as *sanyaasi...* Manu. As such, Ravana is in the getup of an unmistakable Brahman *sanyaasi*, with an unbridled tongue. As with a pitchiest gloom overcoming the sunless and moonless lively eventide, that great-mighty Ravana came over to Vaidehi in that forest, when she is without two of the brothers, namely Rama and Lakshmana. As a sinister planet looks over Star Rohini when she is devoid of Moon, that extremely sinister Ravana then looked over the glorious and youthful princess Sita. Rohini is the principle star and dear wife of the Moon will be in lunar asterism of the same name, and when she comes in the view of planets like Saturn and Mars astrology predicts earthly havocs. Hence, Ravana is compared with such a planet and Sita with Rohini.

The reaction of the trees, wind, and river is as said by gods to Brahma in Bala Kanda, at 1-15-10: "Surya, the Sun will not verily parch Ravana. Maarutha, the Air will not surge at his sides. On seeing Ravana, the lord of the undulating, drifting waves, Ocean... will not pulsate either, and will hide the undulating waves, for the waves are his wives, and Ravana may abduct them... like Sita." This idiomatic usage of *trina kuupa* which draws upon straw, is held high by Dr. Satya Vrat, which is repeated often in Ramayana. He says 'Probably Kalidasa too was inspired by this very expression of Valmiki when he put it in the mouth of Shakuntala as she was being repudiated by Dushyanta: *ko anyo dharma kancuka pravepina tōa kpa upama asya tava anukri bhaviÿyati - abhijñna pkuntalam.* The beautiful outfits on this lotus-stalk like Sita are her *mukha kamala, netra kamala, kara kamala, paada kamala...* 'lotus-eyes, lotus-face, lotus-stalk like hands and lotus-feet and other limbs...' The word *padmini* also means a 'lake' besides the runner of lotus plant. The first compound is also read as: *raupya kaancana aabhaa* meaning 'shining like silver and gold...' but it is in limited mms and with very limited use.

These three attributes are as informed by gods to Vishnu about the three wives of Dasharatha at 1-15-20, as: *hrii, hrillekha,* virtue, modesty, uprightness... *shrii, shriikaara* affluence, prosperity and also suggestive of resplendence, radiance of that prosperity or effluence and *kiirti* fame, renown, glory... a *bhuuti, vibhuuti* is accordance, give-all, fortune. The ash applied on forehead in worships is to be applied with a verse *bhuutir bhuutikar iishvarii...* and for each of these attributes, a presiding deity is there with the same name. Here the *hrii* is also taken to mean *bhuu devi* 'Mother Earth' another wife of Vishnu. The addressing *varaarohe* etc., are the attributes of the addressees as a beautiful woman in the group of: *varaarohaa, matta kaashinii, uttamaa, vara varNiniii - amara kosha* .

Ravana says 'your kind of female is unspotted by me among humans, so you must be some goddess, but I have marked all gods and there I did not find you. This province belongs to demons. As such, gods, *gandharva-s, kinnaraa-s* and others cannot enter this place, let alone the gods from Shiva's side, because Shiva is the Ultimate for demons. If so, do you belong to *ekaa dasha rudraa-s* eleven *Rudraa-*

s? Or, because Air can circulate here, do you belong to any of the forty-nine *marut gaNaa-s*, Wind-gods? Or, because earth has ancient connections with *aSTa vasu-s*, eight-*Vasu-s*, do you belong to any one of them?' Further, Sita is not smiling throughout this conversation as her mind is set on her husband's safety. Nevertheless Ravana assumes that if Sita smiles, that smile will be impeccable.

Did she recognise Ravana as a pseudo-Brahman or not... is the doubt raised by the poet in this verse, because different texts use different compounds *apaaya a darshanam.... upaaya a darshanam* etc. It is concluded that she, for sure, identified him as a pseudo-Brahman, because she has seen many such *sanyaasi-s* while she was in Mithila. Hence she is said here as *Maithili* because she hails from Mithila and her father's court was full with these *sanyaasi-s, yati-s, parivraajaka-s.* Then it is questioned as to why she invited him, though recognised him as a pseudo-Brahman. For this Govindaraja says: *kÿya daõÿa mtreõa yati pjyo na samþaya* 'By spotting the saffron robe alone, a *sanyaasi* is venerable...' Then, another doubt is raised as to how she noticed him to be pseudo- *sanyaasi* . For this it is said *rtri adhvnam ynam ca stry kath laulyam eva ca | mancakam þukla vastram yatynm patanni ÿa ||* 'Walking during night, using vehicles, showing interest in episodes relating to women, and relations with women, using a cot to sleep, wearing white cloths... these six show the downfall of his sanyaasi-hood...' Ravana is indulged in *strii kathaa* in the whole of this chapter, in admiring at her lips, breasts, thighs etc., and no usual *swasti vacana, shubha aashiis* 'blessings...' are uttered by him and thus Sita could discern him to be a pseudo- *sanyaasi.*

Though knowing him as such, why should she revere him at all, is another question. What else she could do as his appearance itself is *uddveSTum a shakyam* 'irrefutable appearance of a Brahman *sanyasi*...' hence, somehow some time is to be gained until the arrival of Rama or Lakshmana. Otherwise, this pseudo-*sanyaasi* may cause any pseudo-problem that she cannot solve. For this, the reply is at the word in the last verse *haritam dadarsha...* 'only greenery is seen by her not Rama nor Lakshmana...' And in the next verse itself she is addressing him as a 'Brahman...' but not with the titles like *sanyasi or yatiishvara, paramahamsa, parivraajaka* etc.

A Brahmin alone is eligible to take up *sanyaasa* 'Hindu-sanyaasi-hood...' not Kshatriya or others. Hence, she concluded him to be Brahman. When once the *sanyaasi*-hood is taken he is no more a Brahman and his bodily being neutralises in the Absolute, and such a *sanyaasi* shall drag on his body, without comfortable bodily needs, until his natural death. But Sita is addressing him contrary to his stance.

Debate of Sita & Ravana before Kidnapping

The debate of Sita and Ravana has started, as Ravana wished to woo Sita. In the first instance Sita believes him to be a Vedic Brahman but insists to know about him. Ravana reveals his identity and asks her to become his wife. Thereupon she goes into a frenzied state and brainstorms Ravana in all her curtness.

When Ravana whose intention is to abduct her has enquired thus, then on the basis of his Brahman friar's mien Sita informed about herself on her own. Thinking briefly that, 'he is a Brahman and an untimely guest, he will indeed curse me if he is not replied,' Sita spoke this sentence.

A lie cannot be uttered to a *sanyaasi*, much less to a *Brahman*. This friar appears as someone who is attired as a *sanyaasi* to fill his stomach. But he is *Brahman*, because he came booming Vedic hymns, which no other lesser *Brahman* can do. Thus, he is someone with a perfect Vedic background... and according to the saying *yatiinaam puujanam kaaryam striyaa vaa puruSena...* 'an ascetic is to be revered either by a lady or a gentleman...' 'and thus he cannot be turned out saying 'my husband is not at home...' 'and if he is neglected he may curse...' these are the criss-cross thoughts of Sita at that moment. Ghastly Viradha boldly carried her off at one time, but she is yet to see the cunningness of a demon. So with a half-belief and half-heart she started to talk to him.

"I am the daughter of noble-souled Janaka, the king of Mithila, by name I am Sita, and the dear wife and queen of Rama, let safety betide you. Here some versions use *bhaaryaa* 'wife' while some use *mahiSii* 'queen...' and this *bhadram te* coupled with *jihiirSuNaa* 'abduction wisher...' is taken as a forewarning to Ravana, as she immediately says who her husband is, as she is aware that this friar is Ravana. Then it implicitly means 'you who wish to abduct me, think twice, for my husband is Rama, and let safety prevail on whole of your dynasty, for it is hard to deal with Rama or with his dear queen-wife...'

"On residing in the residence of Ikshvaku-s in Ayodhya for twelve years, I was in sumptuosity of all cherishes while relishing all humanly prosperities.

Mythically Sita is Goddess Lakshmi and an accorder of prosperity. Here she is saying that she had to enjoy 'humanly indulgences...' because her husband incarnated himself as a man, and since she had to enjoy along with him in her in-law's place, she enjoyed those luxuries. Or, if this is read as *a+ maanuSa bhogaan* 'superhuman delights...' [of course, not 'inhuman delights...'] she enjoyed heavenly comforts as she was enjoying as Lakshmi in *vaikunTha* 'Milky Ocean of Vishnu.' And then, she is indirectly telling Ravana that she has come now as Sita, after immolating herself as Vedavati, in an earlier incarnation, only to end Ravana. "In the thirteenth year the lordly king Dasharatha deliberated together with his imperial ministers to anoint Rama as Crown Prince of Ayodhya."

But lengthy narrations are there in calculating the age of Rama and Sita, at this point of legend with these stanzas. The letter *bha* in the line *mama bhartaa mahaatejaa* is the ninth letter of Gayatri hymn and thus the ninth book of Ramayana with thousand couplets is started from here. The whole of Ramayana is with twenty-four thousand verses and Gayatri hymn has twenty-four letters, and each book of Ramayana contains a thousand verses, starting with each letter of Gayatri. This is the then classification of the cantos of this epic and such grouping of verses is non-existent now. The dexterity of an archer depends mainly on his sighting and targeting eye. Hence, the eyes and dexterity are to be coupled instead of cleaving them as two attributes of Rama. Otherwise, in Sita's saying that 'my husband is a broad-eyed one...' it does not make any sense to Ravana, because Ravana's eyes are much more bigger and bloodshot. Thus 'my ambidextrous husband's eyes are broad *puNDariika vishaala akshaH*, and those eyes are a couple of fish-eye lenses of a camera and can view in 360º, thus you cannot escape their target, in any angle...' Further, these and some more attributes in the coming verses like *simha uraska* etc., they are the very same words coined by Sage Narada, while informing Valmiki about Rama in the first chapter of *Bala Kanda*. Some think such repetitions are essentially Homeric. But in Indian scripts they are not mere repetitions but reiteration of the very same concept in the very same words, which is not an epical flaw in view of the ruling *aadaraat punarukti, aadaraat dvirukti*...'an affectionate reiteration...' Hence, the very same words are put on the tongue of the principle character, Sita. A stepmother is called as *vi maata* or *dvaimaata* and it is said *vaimaatreyo vimaatR^ija - amara kosha* one is other mother, the other is second-mother, both are the nomenclatures of a stepmother. Some texts use the word *brahma caarii* 'celibate' basing on the word Rama used when saying about Lakshmana to Shuurpanakha about Lakshmana as *apuurvii* while some others use as above. She is addressing him as 'oh, Brahman...' and yet asking his caste. This implies her knowledge and/or ignorance about Ravana. As a housewife, it is a natural question to be put to an out-of-way friar moving in the deep of forests. Here, neither a village, nor a single family, nor even a human being is available to accord alms, and this odd almsman is moving here who is supposed to move about villages as said: *bhiksha artham graamam pravishet.* Or, she must be asking him about his caste, creed etc., when he was a householder. But it is out of place. On the other hand, if Sita is from a well-trained family, she is not supposed to question the caste, creed, and name of a real *sanyaasi*. Again, she is asking him to reveal himself 'in essence, truthfully.' She might have thought him to be a cursing Brahman in the first instance, but she might have found him out to be a pseudo-*sanyaasi*. Now that she is slowly realising that he may not be a proper *Brahman* either, she may be asking him straightforwardly. Because Ravana is coming out of Brahman's guise in next two stanzas, it is said that she pointedly asked him as above. Ravana as a devotee of Lakshmi said the above as a renouncer. *tvaam dR^iSTvaa* 'on seeing you...' after a long time...*svakeSu* 'in my kith and kin...' *daareSu* wives...' *ratim* 'pleasure, involvement...' *na adhigacChaami* 'not, I attain...' 'On seeing you, I no longer can attain pleasure with my kith and kin, or with my wives... for I have seen my ultimate motherly goddess... thus I am ready to renounce this accursed being of Ravana...' Maheshvara Tirtha. Ravana as devotee is saying: *aaR^itaanaam uttamam striiNaam* 'To all of the choicest women appropriated by me...; *mama* to me'; *agra mahiSiiyaa* 'to the one who is my prime queen'; *tasyaaH ca mama ca* to her and to me; *bhava iishvarii* you be the ruling deity; 'To all of the choicest women appropriated by me... and to the one who is my present prime queen, namely Mandodari, to her and to me, and to all of us, you be the ruling deity...' *Tiirtha*. The word *bhaamini* is an addressing to a beautiful lady, who is with some anger or resentment *kopanaa saa eva bhaaminii - amara kosha* and Ravana mistook Sita's fury as 'an anger in passion.' Ravana, the devotee, is saying *panca sahasraaNi daasyaH* 'five thousand servants...' *me* 'with me... together with me' *paricariSyasi yadi tava* 'if we all render service to you...' then you will be *baaryaa; bha + aaryaa; bhaayaa= kaantyaa, aaryaa= puujyaa* 'by your splendour...' *bhavasi* you will become the venerable Goddess Lakshmi by your own splendour while thousands are serving you...' Here the word *tu* in *raavaNena evam uktaa tu* is said as *tu shabdena puurvokta upacaara vacana vilakshaNa vacana* it means ultimately as - Sita spoke in derision. 'A mountain will be unswerving even if a hundred thunderbolts strike it at once, thus is my husband... but you, you are always swerving while hankering after your petty cherishes... thus, you are a straw in the wind... my husband is a coequal of Indra, while you are humiliated by Indra's son. The ocean will be turbulent on its surface but it will be calm and clear at its abyss, engulfing unusual treasures... though my husband appears as a passionate person, an indulgent person in humanly pursuits, from hunting games to hollering, in worldly agonies and ecstasies, but at his heart, he is like the fathomless serene ocean... I have avowed to follow him in this lifetime.'

The banyan tree is an Indian fig tree, Ficus benghalensis, the branches of which hang down and root themselves. The simile of a banyan tree to Rama says that: he is an atom in the atomic seed of that tree. On its growth, it spreads so wide and broad and every branch take its own root like the manifold growth of this universe. Hence, every individual being is his offspring and progeny. And the whole universe is pervaded by his 'tree-top' like shelter.

Secondly, that tree gives shelter to innumerable beings for it is so wide at its apex. Hence, anyone can take shelter under Rama, because he is obliged to oblige all *sarva jana anukuulata*as said in an ancient saying: *kpa udakam vaa cchy yuvatynm stana dvayam | þyt kle bhavet uÿõam uÿõa kle bhavet þytalam ||* 'water in a well, banyan tree shade, maiden's two breasts, will warm up in cold season and cool down in hot season...' Govindaraja. The banyan tree is an Indian fig tree, Ficus benghalensis, the branches of which hang down and root themselves. The simile of a banyan tree to Rama says that: he is an atom in the atomic seed of that tree. On its growth, it spreads so wide and broad and every branch take its own root like the manifold growth of th. 'His dexterity is evident from the moment he started to save the order of universe, at the time churning Milky Ocean, becoming Mohini, becoming a Fish, a Tortoise etc. His strides are evident, when he as a dwarfish boy strode all the three worlds. As a lion-man, he tore the very stomach of the evil and now he is striding like a prancing lion towards you, for you alone are the prey for that lionised human incarnation...'

'He is a valiant person and he confronts, if need be, his enemies straightforwardly, about which you have heard when your *Khara*, *Dushana*, and others are eliminated by him... but you are sneaky and slithery... you are ever a thief, never a valiant one... his face is like a pleasant full-moon, at any given opportunity, while yours is revulsive... and you are like the eclipsing planet Rahu or Ketu, whose effect lasts a few minutes... he is expressly acclaimed for his welfare activities and of course, you are also expressly acclaimed, but, only for your ill-faring actives... the senses of an yet to be crowned prince will be like the unbridled horses... but my husband conquered his own senses like an uncrowned sagacious emperor... while you, though you declare yourself as the monarch of demons, there is not even an iota of self-righteousness in you, befitting even to a petty king... then where is the question of your majesty, monarchy, or sovereignty...'

Sita reiterates the statement 'I am avowed to adhere to such a Rama...' four times. This is *daarDhyata* - said for the purpose of 'reinforcement' of her statement.

A fox usually waits in a ditch until the lion or lioness finishes its feast. The lion will have its lion's share and go away. Then the lioness and her cubs have their share and go away. Then it is the day of the fox-in-the-ditch. 'Like a fox-in-the-ditch, how you dare to come to an inaccessible lioness, when the lion departed...' Next, Sun's wife is Prabha or Shine and she is non-figural resplendent entity. She is perceivable but untouchable. If anyone can lay his hands on her by the dint of his yogic or ascetic practises, and if he baskets that Shine for use in night, that night becomes a day, for it will be shining with sunshine, and thus his pleasurable night is evanished. Thereby he loses his minimal personal comfort of a night and it will be self-ruinous to experiment with such ideas.

The simile of lion and serpent is to Rama and the fangs to Sita. A lion or a snake knows well how to protect its instruments, namely fangs. Hence, Sita is the fang of expeditious and ravenous Rama in eliminating evil on earth and now he will become a grudging venomous cobra too, for its tail is going to be trampled, by Sita's abduction. Thus, the instrumentality of Sita is established and no instrument needs to bother on its own, because its owner takes care of that instrument.

She is reminiscing her emergence. Mt. Mandara is mentioned but not Mt. Himalayas or Mt. Meru, even though they are more massive and lofty. Vishnu used Mt. Mandara as a churn-staff when Milk Ocean was churned, but not Himalayas or Meru and the burden of that Mt. Mandara was sustained by Vishnu alone as a Tortoise, which is impossible for simpletons like Ravana, as Ravana failed to lift Mt. Kailash. Before Lakshmi's emergence from the churning Milk Ocean, Her elder sister *haalaahala* 'lethal poison' emerged and it could be contained only by Shiva, and now, if Ravana contemplates to consume her elder sister *kaalakuuTa, haalaahala* 'lethal poison' it is evident what will become of him. This is *nidarshana alankaara; samaanya vaakyaartha aikyata* 'aesthetics of correspondence...'

This declaration that she is selfsame to Rama is on the analogy of *raamaa* the feminal name of Rama. *aham naryany nama s satt vaiÿõavy par-lakÿmy tantra-yah may jagat vyptam svarpeõa svabhvata | tay vptam idam viþvam niyantry ca tath yþvary ||* 'I am indeed Naaraayanee [i.e. Lakshmi] the supreme essence of Lord

Vishnu——Lakshmi Tantra 3.1. 'In my essence and entity I pervade all this universe, and as I pervade all over I am the controller and presiding deity...'

Here, if a fly is accidentally swallowed along with pure ghee, it will be vomited out for the nausea caused by that fly in the stomach. But diamond rends the stomach. The word *vajram* is usually a diamond, and if a diamond is consumed, accidentally or wilfully, it will tear off the intestines to death. Hence taking the Vedic saying *vajro va aajyam* the word is generally translated as ghee.

She poured forth all of her feelings unbothered for consequences and when her haranguing is over, she felt certain uneasiness. This uneasiness is two-fold. One is in accordance with humanly nature of a woman as she is staunch enough to not yield to any, and if anyone makes an untoward advance, she has a 'list' of suicide-programs, those that are narrated to Lakshmana. Further, she is yet to know about Rama's welfare, which will be impossible if this demon carries her away now. On the other side, as a Divine Consort of Vishnu, her uneasiness is for her separation from Rama, but not from the fear of any molestation by Ravana, and as the expected hour has come, the expectancy for the prospective elimination of Ravana is making her to tremble, impetuously.

Rama Laments Sita

In the *Yudh Kanda* of Valmiki Ramayan Rama recollects the lotus-eyed Sita and laments much about his separation from her. Lakshmana consoles him and there approaches the sun-set. That famous army, well-protected by Neela, was kept stationed nicely at the northern shore of the ocean. Both Maina and Dvivida the distinguished monkeys there moved in all directions through that army, for the purpose of vigilance. Rama said that sorrow gets vanished at the passing of time. But my agony of not seeing my beloved is getting increased every day. There is no anguish for me that my beloved is at a distance, nor that she was taken away. Her age is indeed passing away. Only about this, I am repenting. Oh, wind! Flow from the side of my beloved. Touch her and touch me too. It is through you that I get a contact of her limbs. It is through moon that I get a contact of her eyes. That darling being carried away; might have cried "Oh, Lord!" seeking for help. That thought is like poison gulped by me, hovering in my stomach and scorching my limbs. My body is scorching night and day, by the fire of passion, holding fuel of my separation from her and my thoughts of her flaring into shimmering flames." "Oh, Lakshmana! Diving deep into the sea without you, I shall fall asleep. This flaming passion will not thus scorch me, lying down in water. It is enough for me, who is passionate, that Sita with charming thighs and me are resting on one and the same earth and on this fact I am able to survive. When indeed Sita the virtuous lady similar to the child of a celestial, with an excited longing, will embrace my neck and release tears of joy? When shall I thrillingly abandon this terrible anguish, born out of my separation from Sita so soon, as we abandon soiled clothing?" While that sagacious Rama was lamenting thus there, the sun, the weak-rayed due to day-decline, approached the dusk. Lakshmana consoled Rama who was overwhelmed with anguish, duly recollecting the lotus-eyed Sita. Thereafter, Rama worshipped the evening-twilight.

Sita Reply to Rama at the Time of Agni Pariksha

Sita gives a taunting reply to Rama, saying that why she was not abandoned by the latter, even at the time when Hanumana came to see her in Lanka. Then, Sita requests Lakshmana to prepare a pile of fire for her to enter. When Lakshmana prepares a pyre, Sita prays the fire-god and enters into it, in order to prove her conjugal fidelity. Hearing the harsh words with indignation, spoken by Rama, which caused her hair to stand on end, Sita became very much perturbed. Hearing the terrific words of her husband, which were never actually heard by her before, amidst a large gathering of people, Sita stood bent low with shame. As though her own limbs were pierced by those words, which were arrow-like with pointed splinters, Sita shed profuse tears. Then, wiping clean her face, which was bathed in tears, she spoke the following words slowly, in a stammering voice to her husband. Why are you speaking such harsh words, which are violent to hear for me, like a common man speaking to a common woman? I am not the one in the way you understand me. Have a faith in me. I swear to you by my own character." "By the conduct of vulgar woman you distrust the entire race of women. Give up this doubt, if I have been actually tested (and found trustworthy) by you. It was not my willfulness, when I came into contact with the person of Ravana. I was helpless. My adverse fate was to blame on that score." "My heart, which was subservient to me, was abiding in you. What could I do, helpless as I was, with regard to my limbs which had fallen under the sway of another? If I could not be fully known to you, in spite of our love having simultaneously grown and despite of our having lived together, I am ruined permanently by such ignorance." Hanumana, the great hero, was sent by you as your search-agent. Why I, who was still in Lanka, was not abandoned then itself? Life would have been given up by me, when deserted by you; immediately on hearing the message (conveying your desertion) before the eyes of the monkey." "This wasteful endeavour (in the form of crossing over to Lanka and waging war against the mighty Ravana, keeping your life in jeopardy), would not have been there, nor would have your friends been put to such fruitless hardship." You, however, like a feeble man, gave priority to womanliness, conforming yourself to just an emotion of anger. O knower of virtuous conduct! My birth was from Janaka in disguise; but was actually from the earth. My sacred birth of such a high degree was not honoured by you." "My hand taken (by you as a bride) in our childhood was not duly recognized by you. My devotion, my chastity and all have been ignored by you." Sita, thus speaking, weeping and stammering with tears, said to Lakshmana, who was sad and engaged in thoughtfulness: "O Lakshmana! Create a pile of fire, for me, which is a remedy for this disaster. I no longer wish to survive, smitten as am with false blames. I will enter a fire, to obtain the only course appropriate for me, who has been abandoned amidst an assembly of men, by my husband who was not satisfied with my traits." Hearing the words of Sita, Lakshmana, the destroyer of enemy warriors, giving way to wrath, looked towards Rama. Understanding the inclination of the mind of Rama, hinted by the expression in his face, that valiant Lakshmana prepared a pyre, in deference to the wishes of Rama. No one near and dear was indeed able to cajole on that occasion or to speak or even to look upon Rama, who appeared like Yama the lord of death at the time of dissolution of the world. Thereupon, Sita, after doing circumambulation to Rama, who was standing with his head bent low, proceeded towards the blazing fire. Having offered salutation to gods and *brahmins* as also having joined her palms in the vicinity of the fire, Sita spoke the following words: "As my heart never moves off from Rama, so let the fire-god, the witness of the world, protect me from all sides. As Rama apprehends me, though of unimpeachable conduct, to be spoilt, let the fire-god the witness of the world protect me from all sides." "As I have never been unfaithful in act, thought and speech to Rama, who knows all the virtues, so let the fire-god protect me. Since the adorable sun-god, wind-god, the four quarters and even so the moon-god, as also the deity presiding over the day-time and the twilights and the night and the earth and even others know me to be endowed with good conduct, so let the fire-god protect me." Thus speaking, Sita walking around the fire-god, with her mind free from hesitation, entered the blazing fire. A large gathering of men including children and elders saw the shining Sita having entered the fire there. That Sita, with the shining of fresh refined gold and decked with ornaments of refined gold, plunged into the blazing fire, in the presence of all people. All the living beings saw then that wide-eyed Sita, who looked like a golden altar, plunging into the fire. The sages, gods, and the Gandharvas saw that illustrious Sita entering deep into the fire as a sacred oblation of clarified butter. All the women (who were present there) screamed on seeing her, rushing into the fire, like a gush of clarified butter plunging into the sacrificial fire, duly consecrated by Vedic hymns. The denizens of the entire three worlds including the gods, Gandharvas and demons, beheld her falling into the fire, like a goddess, subjected to a curse, falling from heaven to hell. While she was entering deeply into the fire, a loud sound, which appeared strange, uttering 'Alas, Alas' rose both from the demons and the monkeys alike.

9

An Unfair World for the Fair Sex

In modern days inadequate work place policies and unequal family responsibilities have made it difficult for women to make a mark. Women face a trade-off between competence and likeability in circumstance where effective leadership requires both. A cottage industry of studies makes clear that women's under-representation in leadership positions is at least partly attribut-able to traditional gender expectations and practices.

विपदि धैर्यमथाभ्यूदये क्षमा सदसि वस्कपदुता यूधि विक्रमः।

यशसि चाभिरूचि र्व्यसनं श्रुतो प्रकृति सिद्धमिदं हि महात्मनाम् ।।

Courage in adversity, patience in propsertiy, oratory in assembly, bravery in battle, modesty in fame, attachment to knowledge, all these are naturally found in the great persons.

There are few women among today's recognized young women leaders on top position in India. We have to take proactive steps in order to encourage women to continue in the corporate world. We see drop offs happening when they get married, move with spouses to different locations and when they have children. We have to change the perspective of society. In India it is very important to say that working women should continue to be engaged. A cultural change is required both of corporate and individual level. Companies need to do a lot more. They create a special flexibility for women almost as a compulsory standard.

Marissa Mayer was hired as Yahoo CEO when she was six month pregnant. Mayer did not take maternity leave and worked throughout. She delivered a baby boy and surprisingly next day she was involved in critical decision of Yahoo and she returned office in 1-2 weeks time. Mayer work is hard to emulate in India where women have greater cultural and family pressures and companies are less flexible in helping women balance life and career. Indian CEO's are speaking up now. Companies need more sensitivity in imagination for women to rise to the top.

Initially, the hope was that filling the pipeline would take care of the problem, but it is now clear that time alone is not the answer. For more than two decades, women have been earning about one-third of the MBAs awarded in the US, and other countries yet they constitute less percentage of Fortune CEOs and top leadership position. These statistics point to the barriers women face in gaining leadership roles, but traditional gender expectations and practices also shape people's experiences even after they reach the top. A fundamental challenge to women's. leadership arises from the mismatch between the qualities traditionally associated with leaders and those traditionally associated with women. The assertive, authoritative and dominant behaviours that people link with leadership tend not to be viewed as attractive in women.

Although attitudes toward women as a group are generally positive, even more positive than attitudes toward men, these views do not hold for women who occupy traditionally male roles, especially when they excel in those roles. When women achieve in distinctly male arenas, they are seen as competent but are less well liked than equally successful men. By the same token, when women performing traditionally male roles are seen as nice, they are liked but not respected. In short, women, unlike men, face trade-offs between competence and like abil-ity in traditionally male roles.

In leadership contexts, these biases play out on several levels: in the ways that organizations structure leadership paths and positions, in the ways that people perceive women leaders, and in the ways that women leaders perceive themselves and what they must do to succeed. At each level, a woman's qualifications for leadership are called into question. Differential structures of opportunity and power block women's access and advancement to leadership positions. For example, men's predominance in positions of organizational power, together with difference in the composition of men's and women's social and professional networks, gives men greater access to information and support. Women in traditionally male-dominated setting often have difficulty breaking into 'old boys' loop of advice and professional de-velopment opportunities. Isolation and exclusion are particularly likely for women of colour.

The problem of exclusion is compounded by organizational structures and practices that tend to reflect and support men's experiences. For example, women are disadvantaged by the convergence of their biological and professional clocks and by the escalating time demands of leadership positions. The increasing pace and competitiveness of organizational life, coupled with technological advances, have created a culture of constant accessibility and blurred the boundaries of home and work. Although technology has made it easier for a woman to work from home, it has also made it harder not to. Excessive hours are a major reason that many highly qualified women step off the leadership track.

Although men have assumed an increasing share of house hold re-sponsibilities over the last quarter century, women continue to shoulder the major burden, Women put in about twice as much time on childcare as men. In a study involving well-educated profes-sional women who had left the paid workforce, two-thirds cited their husbands' role as a reason for the decision, including their lack of support in childcare and other domestic tasks, and their expectation that wives should be the ones to cut back on employment.

Unlike most male leaders, most aspiring female leaders lack the support of spouses who are full time homemakers or who are working only part-time. Women with families also face more constraints on travel and relocation than similarly situated men. Until the home becomes an equal opportunity employer, women will pay the price in the world outside it. Employment policies reflect and further reinforce gender differences in family roles and responsibilities. Most workplaces fail to offer the same paid parental leave to fathers as to mothers, and few men take any extended period of time away from jobs for family reasons.

Related problems stem from the lack of flexible schedules, meaningful part-time positions and affordable quality childcare. Although women in top managerial and professional positions often are in workplaces that offer reduced or flexi-time arrangements, few of these women take advantage of them. Most believe, with reason, that any limitation in hours or availability would jeopardize their careers, and that they would end up w6rkingmore than their status and compensation justified.

These inadequate workplace policies and unequal family responsibilities help account for gender differences in paid leadership positions. Women with graduate or professional degrees have stepped out of the labour force, compared with imilarly credentialed men. In organizations with few if any women in positions of power, gender is particularly salient and negatively affects women lower in the ranks, despite balanced representation at those levels.

Women are becoming more like men in their career aspirations and achievements and are more willing to see themselves as having charac-teristics associated with authority. So, too, recent theories of leadership have stressed the importance of interpersonal qualities commonly attributed to women, such as co-operation, collaboration and interpersonal sensitivity. An emerging body of scholarship suggests that the most effective style of leadership in today's world is 'transformational'. Leaders who take this approach em-phasize gaining the trust and confi-dence of followers and empowering them to develop their own potential. Meta-analyses of studies involving thousands of leaders suggest that women are somewhat more transformational than men, especially in providing support for subordinates.

Yet despite these trends, the legacy of traditional gender stereotypes remains. Women have long suffered from a double standard and double bind in the exercise of authority. They are thought too aggressive or not aggressive enough, and what appears assertive, in a man appears abrasive in a woman. As noted above, women who conform to traditional feminine stereotypes are often liked but not respected: they are judged too soft, emotional and unassertive to make tough calls and project the necessary 'presence' in positions of authority.

By contrast, women who adopt more masculine traits are often respected but not liked: they are seen as domineering, strident and cold. Self-promoting behaviour that appears self-confident or entrepreneurial in men often looks pushy and 'unfeminine' in women. In effect, women face a trade-off between competence and likeability in circumstances where effective leadership requires both.

Recent research suggests that two co-existing and complementary forms of sexism-one benevolent and the other one hostile-lie at the root of this dilemma. Benevolent sexism is "a subjectively favour-able, chivalrous ideology that offers protection and affection to women who embrace conventional roles" and is used to reward women who conform to traditional gender role expectations. Hostile sexism is "antipathy toward women who are viewed as usurping men's power" and is used to punish women who challenge the status quo. Taken together, these prejudices reflect ambivalence about women, promoting polarized responses to them.

This double bind helps account for why women continue to be rated lower than men on most of the qualities associated with leadership. People more readily credit men with leadership ability and more readily accept men as leaders. The presence of a few highly regarded women at the top creates the illusion that the glass ceiling has been shattered for everyone else. But when superstars fail or opt out, their departures attract particular notice and reinforce stereotypes about women's lesser capabilities and commitment.

Ability has got Nothing to do with Success

There is a strong tendency to attribute our successes and failures to ability. And by that we usually mean some innate quality or aptitude. So you either win the DNA lottery and end up with lots of intelligence or creativity or willpower and are therefore successful, or you don't, and you fail. This simplistic explanation is wrong for two reasons. First, ability simply doesn't work that way. No matter which ability you are talking about-whether it's intelligence, creativity, athletic prowess or self-control research shows them to be malleable. In other words, no matter what you start with, what you end up with has everything to do with experience, learning and effort. If you want to be smarter, you can get smarter. When we think of our abilities as fixed and innate, we give up on ourselves when we encounter difficultly, and resign ourselves to failure.

The second reason why this explanation is wrong is that no matter how much ability you have, successfully reaching a goal has everything to do the actions you take (or don't take) along the way. Effort, strategy, mindset, motivation, confidence, planning and monitoring of progress are the true keys to achievement, and they are much more powerful than 'ability' or 'aptitude'. But until we start rejecting explanations like "I'm just not smart enough" or "I don't have what it takes", we won't start looking for the real problems, and figuring out solutions.

To explain success (and failure), we need to look to our actions, rather than our abilities. We need to think about the aspects of our performance that are under our control the effort we put in, the strategies we used, the critical steps we may have neglected, whether or not we considered the obstacles to success, etc.

Ability is a very poor predictor of success-measures like IQ don't do a very good job of telling us who will perform well at work and who will perform poorly. Again, it comes down to doing the right things-abilities are expressed through our actions. Sometimes, people are too quick to give up on themselves when work becomes difficult, while others persist and double their efforts. It's the latter who will succeed.

Self-confidence, belief in the ability to improve, patience and persistence these are inherent in a successful individuals. The good news is, none of these traits are innate-we can develop these through experience and effort.

Ref: *Hand book of leadership theory*, Published by Harvard Business Press.

End